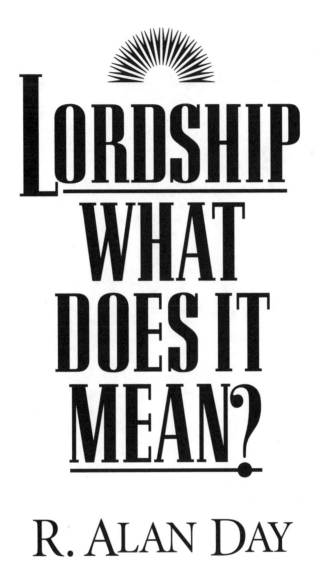

LORDSHIP WHAT DOES IT MEAN?

R. ALAN DAY

BROADMAN PRESS
NASHVILLE, TENNESSEE

© Copyright 1993 • Broadman Press
All Rights Reserved
4281-57

IBSN: 8054-8157-5
Dewey Decimal Classification: 234
Subject Heading: SALVATION
Library of Congress Catalog Number: 92-30030
Printed in the United States of America

Library of Congress Cataloging-in-Publication Data

Day, R. Alan. 1948-
    Lordship—what does it mean? / R. Alan Day.
    p. cm.
    Includes bibliographic references.
    ISBN 0-8054-8157-5
    1. Salvation. 2. Commitment to the church. 3. Christian life-Baptist authors. I. Title.
    BT752.D39 1992   92-30030
    234—dc20   CIP

Table of Contents

Dedication

To the loving churches who have allowed me to be their pastor:
Oak Grove Baptist Church, Bentley, Louisiana
Emmanuel Baptist Church, Bunkie, Louisiana
Gray's Creek Baptist Church, Denham Springs, Louisiana
Golden Acres Baptist Church, Pasadena, Texas
First Baptist Church, McComb, Mississippi
First Baptist Church, Edmond, Oklahoma

Introduction

This book began over twenty years ago when I was a student at Louisiana College. A friend gave me a copy of Dietrich Bonhoeffer's *The Cost of Discipleship,* and I made the mistake of reading it. I have never quite been the same since.

Until then I had never thought much of the concept of discipleship. To me a disciple was one of the original followers of our Lord, in particular, the original twelve. The idea that Christ calls all of His followers to be disciples had never taken hold in my mind. That is not to say that I did not have a notion of what commitment was all about. I was already disillusioned with much of the cultural Christianity that I was witnessing. I had already begun to preach against the shallow, easy believism that had been popular in evangelicalism for many years. Yet until I read Bonhoeffer, I had never read anyone who gave such full expression to my budding sentiments, and who did it in such a stinging and prophetic way.

Listen to Bonhoeffer's rebuke of what he called "cheap grace":

That is what we mean by cheap grace, the grace which amounts to the justification of sin without the justification of the repentant sinner who departs from sin and from whom sin departs. Cheap grace is not the kind of forgiveness of sin which frees us from the toils of sin. Cheap grace is the preaching of forgiveness without requiring repentance, baptism without church discipline, Communion without confession. Cheap grace is grace without discipleship, grace without the cross, grace without Jesus Christ, living and incarnate.[1]

Early on in my ministry I began to develop some concerns that have stayed with me through these years. One concern is that the lives of many professing believers are not substantially different from those of unbelievers. According to a Gallup Poll, fifty million Americans eighteen years of age and older, claim to have committed themselves to Christ. One would think that with this great number of true believers pornography would not be on the rise, drug-related problems would be diminishing, and the divorce rate would be abating. However, this is not the case. Surveys indicate that the youth in evangelical churches are experimenting with sex at nearly the same rate as their non-Christian counterparts.

A reporter asked George Gallup why our society is not morally stronger than it is when there are so many people who claim they have been born again. Gallup responded, *"There is a huge gap between mere belief, and real conviction and practice."*[2]

What about those fifty million people who claim to be followers of Jesus Christ? Are they really saved? Can one really be a Christian and live an entire life that is not markedly different from the rest of th world? Is it possible that what we call a "Christian" and what the New Testament calls a "Christian" are not the same things? Is it possible that our easy believism and shallow evangelism have produced a crop of professing believers who have never really entered into a vital relationship with Jesus Christ? On the other hand, is a low standard of commitment to be expected from the multitude of professing Christians? Should we grudgingly acknowledge that few Christians will ever take seriously the demands of the gospel and that most Christians, saved and heaven-bound though they are, will live substantially on the same plane as their pagan counterparts?

Now those kind of questions have been stirring me for these twenty-plus years. More recently an intense debate has broken out within the evangelical community that shows no sign of abating. The controversy is over what is called "Lordship Salvation." The debate goes back to the 1950s when Everett F.

Harrison and John R. W. Stott debated the issue in *Eternity* magazine. The current controversy involves three leading actors: Charles C. Ryrie and Zane C. Hodges on the one side, and John F. MacArthur, Jr., on the other.[3]

Ryrie and Hodges argue that Jesus can be Savior without being Lord. Must persons totally dedicate their lives to Christ or be committed to living a certain life-style before being saved? According to Ryrie and Hodges, to teach this is confusion of salvation and distortion of grace. These men are concerned primarily for the purity and simplicity of the gospel, viz., that Jesus Chris saves by His grace in response to our faith alone.

On the other side of the debate is John MacArthur whose book *The Gospel According to Jesus* is a lengthy response to the writings of Ryrie and Hodges. MacArthur contends that faith is more than intellectual assent to the facts of the gospel, and that submission or dedication and repentance issuing in a life of holiness and commitment are essential to salvation.

The purpose of this book is not to analyze fully the writings of the aforementioned authors. Nor do I want to identify with either side of the controversy. I call attention to the current debate merely to demonstrate that the subject is relevant and very much in the forefront. I will cite relevant statements from their writings to clarify the issue. There is always a tendency to overstate one's point in the heat of controversy. It is possible that Ryrie, Hodges, and MacArthur have all done this. Perhaps if they would sit down across a table and talk, they would not be so far apart as their books seem to indicate.

Nevertheless, the issues are real. Nothing could be more important than the question: What is the gospel? How are persons saved? What is the nature of Christian commitment? Is it possible that many have made decisions, have believed intellectually, and yet are not really "in Christ"? These are some of the issues that we will wrestle with in this brief book.

The principles that guide my study are the absolute authority, trustworthiness, and infallibility of the Bible, a desire to honor Christ as King of kings and Lord of lords, and a heart hunger for a revived church that will preach a pure gospel that our old sin-cursed world so desperately needs.

I offer this book with a prayer that Jesus, the Lord of the church, will use it to stir up His people in this final decade of the twentieth century.

—R. Alan Day

1. Dietrich Bonhoeffer, *The Cost of Discipleship* (New York: Macmillan, Co., Inc., 1963), 47.

2. Quoted by Gary R. Collins in *Beyond Easy Believism* (Waco: Word, Inc., 1982), 10.

3. See the article "How Faith Words" by S. Lewis Johnson, Jr., in *Christianity Today,* September 22, 1989, 21-25.

Easy Believism

Throughout this land there are churches pastored by dynamic communicators who avoid references to sin or failure, and who build their popular sermons around inspiring stories of personal triumph and the value of a positive mental attitude. These churches preach a religion which is easy, convenient, and comfortable. The idea of "sin" has vanished, and with it, words like "self-discipline," "commitment," "repentance," and "sacrifice" have disappeared from the vocabulary and thinking of many modern worshipers and their leaders. When there is no emphasis on repentance, and little emphasis on holiness and the Word of God, there is no true religion. Easy believism reigns instead.

—Gary R. Collins[1]

Many people think that when we preach salvation, we mean salvation from going to hell. We do not [sic] mean that, but we mean a great deal more; we preach salvation from sin; we say that Christ is able to save a man; and we mean by that that he is able to save him from sin and to make him holy; to make him a new man. No person has any right to say, "I am saved," while he continues in sin as he did before. How can you be saved from sin while you are living in it? A man that is drowning cannot say he is saved from the water while he is sinking in it; a man that is frost-bitten cannot say, with any truth, that he is saved from the cold while he is stiffened in the wintry blast. No, man, Christ did not come to save thee in thy sins, but to save thee from thy sins;

11

not to make the disease so that it should not kill thee, but to let it remain in itself mortal, and, nevertheless, to remove it from thee, and thee from it. Christ Jesus came then to heal us from the plague of sin, to touch us with his hand and say, "I will, be thou clean."

—Charles Haddon Spurgeon[2]

1 Easy Believism

In every generation the church must face the question, What is the gospel? The church may be wrong about many issues; but if she is wrong about this essential question, she guarantees her failure. Along with this basic question is another: How much does one have to know and to what does one need to commit in order to receive the gift of salvation?

Through the years I have heard many Christians give testimonies similar to the following: "I was saved when I was sixteen, but I never really committed my life to Christ until now." I have heard that story repeated in many different forms, but the underlying assumption is always the same: One can receive Jesus Christ as Savior (that is, one can intellectually commit oneself to the facts of the gospel) without being committed to Him as Lord of life.

Now what about those who are supposedly "saved" but *never* totally commit their lives to Christ? Are they saved because of their one-time decision "receiving Christ" or "accepting Jesus into their hearts"? Or is it possible that these Christians were not saved in the first place but only later, when they totally committed their lives to Jesus Christ? Does that mean that persons who make shallow commitments, based only upon intellectual assent to the gospel, are not really saved? These are the issues that we want to address in this chapter.

What is Easy Believism?

The term *easy believism* has come to refer to the notion that all that is required of one to be saved is to believe the facts of the gospel. These persons believe the facts that Jesus Christ, the divine Son of God, died on the cross for our sins, was buried and raised the third day. Believing this and in some way expressing their belief to the Lord supposedly constitute the salvation experience. Faith and works are so incongruous that, not only do works contribute nothing to salvation, but no commitment of any kind is required for salvation. No change is called for, since we are saved by "simple naked faith." Some new converts may experience a radical change, but others may not. That is not the issue. The issue for the proponents of "easy believism" is simply: "believe the gospel."

There seems to be confusion over what it means to believe or have faith. The Reformers distinguished between three aspects of faith: knowledge, assent, and trust. *Knowledge* refers to an intellectual understanding of the facts of the gospel; *assent* means that one agrees with the facts of the gospel; and *trust* means that one commits oneself to the Christ of the gospel and the Gospel of Christ. The Reformers understood clearly that "believing" is not just understanding the gospel or assenting to the gospel. One does not believe until committing self to Christ.

John Calvin, for instance, taught that faith always issues in repentance, which he saw as a part of regeneration. When one believes the gospel and trusts Christ, Calvin taught, that person turns from sin to Christ, mortifying the old flesh and the old man by the renewing work of the Holy Spirit. Timothy George wrote, "Calvin would not be pleased with the kind of evangelism which preaches an easy believism, which calls for a decision for Christ without radical, life-changing consequences."[3]

From time to time in history, the church has faced the issue of easy believism or only believism in one form or another. In the middle of the eighteenth century, Scottish preacher Robert Sandeman taught that saving faith is merely believing facts about Christ's atoning death. To believe, according to Sandeman, is simply to be persuaded that the event of Christ's death actually happened as taught in the New Testament. He taught that it is a corruption of the gospel to require repentance and an exercise of the affections. The net result was an absolute intellectualizing of evangelical faith.[4]

Of course, Sandeman was wrong. Baptist Andrew Fuller, among others, used all of his preaching and writing skills to oppose Sandeman. Fuller recognized that if this doctrine caught on, the result would be spiritual death in the church.

Hodges and Ryrie

No one today is saying exactly what Sandeman said, but some are getting dangerously close. Both Zane Hodges and Charles Ryrie suggest, for instance, that the salvation issue is not repentance and change of heart, in regard to a former life-style, but merely believing Jesus is the Christ, the Messiah and the Savior. Both Hodges and Ryrie use the story of the Samaritan woman in John 4 as an example of salvation without commitment.

Hodges wrote:

It must be emphasized that there is no call here for surrender, submission, acknowledgement of Christ's Lordship, or anything else of this kind. A gift is being offered to one totally unworthy of God's favor. And to get it, the woman is required to make no spiritual commitment whatsoever. She is merely invited to ask. It is precisely this impressive fact that distinguishes the true Gospel from all its counterfeits. Did the woman therefore simply return to her former sinful lifestyle? The Scripture does not tell us. It is not at all the point of the story![5]

Ryrie made the exact same claim:

Or what about the Samaritan woman with whom the Lord conversed at Jacob's well? What requirements did He lay on her? She had had five husbands or men, and the one with whom she was living was not her husband. Plainly, she was living in sin. What an opportunity for the Lord to inject the matter of willingness to leave that immoral relationship in order to have living water (eternal life). What a great case study this woman could have been for all mastery advocates from that time to this. But He had already told her what was necessary for her to have living water

(John 4:10)—to know the gift (not reward) of God, and who He was; then ask Him for that water. Even after some of the details of her sordid past and present came to light, Jesus did not change His message. He did allow her to sidetrack Him with her question about where to worship, but He led that part of the dialogue back to the fact that He was the promised Messiah (verse 26). The Bible does not tell us whether or not the woman left her live-in man and mended her ways, but the record is crystal clear as to how she could have eternal life. Receive the gift of eternal life by asking Christ for it.[6]

Both of these reputable scholars made the astounding claim that this woman could have met Jesus, could have seen in Him the Messiah, and could have been born again by the Spirit of God without an inward transformation or repentance that would have led her instinctively and immediately to change her lifestyle. This appeals to silence in the text and seems to ignore some details of the text.

First of all, from the text it is obvious that Jesus directed the conversation so that the woman would be confronted with her sin. The Lord said to her, "Go, call your husband, and come here" (v. 16). Our Lord's intention was obvious: He wanted her to know that He knew her and knew of her sinful past. He had come to be a Savior from sin, and He wanted her to face her sin. If His only purpose had been to show His supernatural knowledge, He could have chosen incidents from her life that had nothing to do with her sinfulness. His motive, however, was to bring her face-to-face with her sinful life-style. Jesus confronted her with her sin and called her to repentance. Furthermore, to say that Jesus did not make commitment or repentance an issue is to build an argument on silence, for we know that their conversation must have lasted longer and covered more details than those John recorded.

John does not tell us whether or not the woman truly believed. It seems obvious that she did because she was so excited and went and told the men (who knew her all too well) that she had met a man who had told her everything she had ever done. She seems to have been changed, and that change would mean repentance from her former life-style. It is unthinkable that she would have returned that night to her immoral relationship or would have gone immediately back into a life of sin. It is beyond me how two reputable theologians could even suggest the possibility! Being saved is not merely believing the facts of the gospel. It is believing on or in a Person, the Lord Jesus Christ. When one is saved, the Holy Spirit comes to live in that person; he or she becomes a new creation. No one has ever been saved without recognizing himself or herself as sinful and understanding that Christ died for sinners. That does not mean that one must be a theologian in order to be saved or be able to give a dictionary definition of repentance or faith.

The woman at the well knew that she was sinful, and the Lord Jesus led her to face her sin. In order to accept His offer of salvation, she had to reject her former life-style.

Was Simon the Sorcerer a Christian?

Is it possible to "believe" without really being saved? Yes, if by *believe* we mean believing only intellectually. In Acts 8, we find the interesting episode of Simon the sorcerer, whom Luke tells us "believed." Simon was baptized and remained with Philip observing his signs and miracles (v. 13). Simon was used to dabbling in certain kinds of magic and was captivated by the miracle-working power of the apostles. After several days, his lust for spiritual power was fully aroused, and he offered money to Peter in exchange for the power to perform miracles. Peter's response is both shocking and instructive:

May your silver perish with you, because you thought you could obtain the gift of God with money! You have no part or portion in this matter, for your heart is not right before God. Therefore repent of this wickedness of yours, and pray the Lord that if possible, the intention of your heart may be forgiven you. For I see that you are in the gall of bitterness and in the bondage of iniquity (vv. 20-23).

Like many people, Simon made a profession of faith. He believed the basics of the gospel. Peter's harsh words indicate that Simon had not yet been converted. To speak of one "in the gall of bitterness and in the bondage of iniquity" is to say that he or she is not yet born again. Simon had obviously made a shallow profession of faith and yet never experienced the regenerating work of the Holy Spirit. Peter did not know this until he observed Simon's life-style, heard his words, and understood his motives.

This is always the case in conversion. Whenever someone professes faith in Christ, it is not yet obvious whether or not the profession of faith is genuine. Only God sees the heart. Yet time will tell. If no change occurs in the person's life, obviously that one has not truly been born again. The person may have "believed" but did not exercise saving faith. This true faith involves not only knowledge and assent but trust, that is, commitment to Christ.

Notice Peter's words to Simon, "Therefore repent of this wickedness of yours" (v. 22). Though Simon had believed intellectually, he had never experienced repentance. It is impossible to be saved unless one repents of sin.

What Is Faith?

The Reformers taught that we are saved by faith alone, but the faith that saves is never alone. In other words, it is accompanied by repentance and a changed life. Easy believism, which emphasizes intellectually embracing the gospel without a change of heart and a deep, inner desire to please the Lord Christ, is a corruption of the gospel.

We must say loudly and clearly that it is not enough simply to believe that Jesus is the Incarnate Son of God who died for our sins. Perhaps many professing Christians today think that is all required for them to get to heaven. Yet Jesus said, "Not everyone who says to Me, 'Lord, Lord,' will enter the kingdom of heaven; but he who does the will of My Father who is in heaven" (Matt. 7:21).

John Stott put it succinctly:

Christianity is no mere passive acquiescence in a series of propositions, however true. We may believe in the deity and the salvation of Christ, and acknowledge ourselves to be sinners in need of his salvation; but this does not make us Christian. There is a personal response which we must make to Jesus Christ, committing ourselves unreservedly to Him as our Saviour and Lord."[7]

Stott wrote further that when Jesus "offered mankind his salvation, He demanded their submission. Jesus gave no encouragement whatever to thoughtless applicants for discipleship."[8] The gospel is, "Believe on the Lord Jesus Christ, and thou shalt be saved" (Acts 16:31, KJV). The Holy Spirit convicts of sin (John 16:8), bringing the repentant sinner to confess Christ's lordship (1 Cor. 12:3). When real faith is present, there will be submission and dedication. There will be a willingness to obey. That is what Bonhoeffer meant when he said, *"Only he who believes is obedient, and only he who is obedient believes."*[9] This is not to say that when persons come to Christ they understand all the issues of discipleship. For instance, a nine-year-old will not understand that the call to be a disciple is the call to sexual purity. This child could not yet understand that issue. Still nine-year-olds who come to Christ put themselves into the hands of the Lord Jesus. They are willing to commit their total life to Christ as Lord and Savior. This initial commitment becomes the basis for further commitments as new issues arise and as new temptations assault.

I do not mean that new believers will be perfect. They will fall again and again, but their tendency is toward holiness. They desire purity. Because they have new hearts, they will never again be the same. The main issue has been settled. They are committed to Christ, who died for them and rose again. They are experiencing in this life the resurrection power that alone can break the shackles of sin.

Yes, we should be careful not to distort the gospel by adding anything to it. Still, easy believism goes the opposite direction:

easy believism reduces faith to mere intellectual assent. I fear that many in the organized church today have "believed" in that sense and yet still never been born again.

May preachers call their people not only to the gospel but to the Christ of the gospel. May God grant us a revival of evangelical repentance!

1. Gary R. Collins, *Beyond Easy Believism* (Waco, Tex.: Word, Inc., 1982), 17.

2. Charles H. Spurgeon, *The Metropolitan Tabernacle Pulpit,* vol. XI (Pasadena, Tex.: Pilgrim Publications, 1970), 138.

3. Timothy George, *Theology of the Reformers* (Nashville: Broadman Press, 1988), 226.

4. See J. I. Packer, "History Repeats Itself," *Christianity Today,* September 22, 1989, 22. Also D. M. Loyd-Jones, "Sandemanianism," *The Puritans: Their Origins and Successors* (Carlisle, Pa.: Banner of Truth Trust, 1987), 170-90.

5. Zane C. Hodges, *The Gospel Under Siege* (Dallas: Redención Viva, 1981), 14-15.

6. Charles C. Ryrie, *So Great Salvation* (Wheaton: Victor Books, 1989), 110-11.

7. John R. W. Stott, *Basic Christianity* (Downers Grove, Il.: Inter-Varsity Press, 1958), 109.

8. Ibid.

9. Dietrich Bonhoeffer, *The Cost of Discipleship* (New York: Macmillan Co., Inc., 1963), 69.

Is Repentance a Part of the Gospel?

But the acceptance of the supernatural depends upon a conviction of the reality of sin. Without the conviction of sin there can be no appreciation of the uniqueness of Jesus; it is only when we contrast our sinfulness with His holiness that we appreciate the gulf which separates Him from the rest of the children of men. And without the conviction of sin there can be no understanding of the occasion for the supernatural act of God; without the conviction of sin, the good news of redemption seems to be an idle tale.

—J. Gresham Machen[1]

The Gospel must be the bad news of the conviction of sin before it can be the good news of redemption. Because that message is unpalatable for many middle-class congregations preoccupied with protecting their affluent life-styles, many pastors endowed with a normal sense of self-preservation tiptoe warily round the subject.

—Charles W. Colson[2]

2 Is Repentance a Part of the Gospel

What is the gospel? Certainly there could be no more important question for Christians to answer. If we may divide the gospel into God's part and our part (what God has done and what God commands for us to do), there is little debate about God's part. Paul outlined the gospel in 1 Corinthians 15:1-5:

> Now I make known to you, brethren, the gospel which I preached to you, which also you received, in which also you stand, by which also you are saved, if you hold fast the word which I preached to you, unless you believed in vain. For I delivered to you as of first importance what I also received, that Christ died for our sins according to the Scriptures, and that He was buried, and that He was raised on the third day according to the Scriptures, and that He appeared to Cephas, then to the twelve.

This is the essence of the gospel. Christ has died for our sins. That great definition of the gospel assumes that we understand more about concepts such as justification, propitiation, sin, and the Law. Yet, this shorthand form of the gospel adequately expresses what God has done to reconcile a lost world to Himself.

What about our part? This is where disagreement comes. Is our part to believe only, that is, to intellectually assent to the facts of the gospel? Or, is there to be repentance? And what exactly is repentance? Does it involve emotion? Is there to be sorrow for sin? Is commitment or turning from a previous life-style a part of repentance?

Concerning this issue, we find a great deal of debate and disagreement. According to Charles Ryrie,

"Paul wrote clearly that the Gospel that saves is believing that Christ died for our sins and rose from the dead. This is the complete Gospel, and if so, then it is also the true full Gospel and the true whole Gospel. Nothing else is needed for the forgiveness of sins and the gift of eternal life."[3]

With this, of course, we would be in agreement. The gospel is that Christ died for our sins and rose the third day.

What about people's response to the gospel? What must they do to be saved?

Ryrie wrote further:

The good news is that Christ has done something about sin and that He lives today to offer His forgiveness to me. The direction is from Christ to me. It is never from me to Him. I do not offer Him anything. How could I? What could I possibly offer that would help meet my need? To offer the years of my life is to offer something very imperfect and something which can do nothing to forgive my sin. To vow my willingness to change is to affirm something I will not consistently keep; and even if I could, it would not remove the guilt of my sin.[4]

Ryrie's meaning is unmistakable. To be saved one simply believes the gospel about the atoning death of Christ. There can be no question of commitment, dedication, forsaking of sin and turning from a former life, a promise to do better, or sorrow over a previously sinful life. In Ryrie's thinking, that would be to add works to grace. It would be unthinkable. We offer God nothing. We receive His gift unconditionally, without any promise on our part to change, to do better, or to be a different kind of person.

Ryrie presents no new doctrine. As noted in the previous chapter, the Scottish preacher, Robert Sandeman, in the middle of the eighteenth century, preached a doctrine of salvation similar to the easy believism of our day. Sandeman believed that it was legalistic to add anything to salvation other than faith, that is, simple intellectual belief in the facts of the gospel. Sandeman rejected the Westminster Confession with its emphasis on believing from the heart. He rejected the teachings of the Puritans, and the preaching of Whitefield and Wesley, who emphasized repentance and godly sorrow as concomitant to saving faith. Sandeman taught that one is saved by "naked faith" without any conviction of sin, without a broken heart, and without repentance. He said that assurance was simply an objective and logical matter having nothing to do with feelings. You need only go to the Scriptures and logically determine whether or not you have done what the Scriptures say. There need be no manifestation of the Holy Spirit or inward witness or testimony of the Holy Spirit. Sandeman feared that to introduce feelings would be to reintroduce the Law, and, thus, corrupt the gospel.[5]

I can understand Sandeman's concern that we not corrupt the gospel. That was the issue in the Jerusalem conference concerning the Judaizers (Acts 15:1-29). We dare not corrupt the gospel; on the other hand, we dare not truncate the message of the gospel and produce "believers" who are intellectually committed to Christ or the gospel but who have never been regenerated by the work of the Holy Spirit.

"What saith the scripture?" (Rom. 4:3, KJV). How did biblical characters handle the issue of repentance? How did the apostles preach the gospel? When we can answer these questions, we will have our gospel for today.

John the Baptist came to pave the way for the ministry of our Lord Jesus. His message was simple, "Repent, for the kingdom of heaven is at hand" (Matt. 3:2). John's place in the economy of God was to help prepare Israel for the coming of the Messiah. He understood that, before Israel would be willing to receive Christ, they must experience a spiritual renewal through their repentance of sins. It is interesting to note that the disciples of John made good disciples of our Lord. Further, there is no indication that anyone who rejected the message of John the Baptist ever accepted the message of Christ.

Then there is the teaching of our Lord Himself. Jesus' first public message was, "Repent, for the kingdom of heaven is at hand" (Matt. 4:17). In Luke 5:32, our Lord warned the Pharisees, "I have not come to call the righteous but sinners to repentance." After Jesus' resurrection, He said to some of the disciples, "Thus it is written, that the Christ should suffer and rise again from the dead the third day; and that repentance for forgiveness of sins should be proclaimed in His name to all the nations, beginning from Jerusalem" (Luke 24:46-47).

The preaching of the disciples included the message of repentance. Before Pentecost the disciples preached "that men should repent" (Mark 6:12). After Pentecost, their message was the same. The first gospel sermon preached after the resurrection of our Lord included the admonition, "Repent, and let each of you be baptized in the name of Jesus Christ for the forgiveness of your sins" (Acts 2:38). In Acts 3:19, again Peter declared, "Repent therefore and return, that your sins may be wiped away." In Acts 5:31, Peter said, "He is the one whom God exalted to His right hand as a Prince and a Savior, to grant repentance to Israel, and forgiveness of sins."

Was the message of repentance limited to the preaching of Peter? Certainly not. In Acts 20:21, the apostle Paul summarized what he had been preaching in Ephesus and elsewhere as "solemnly testifying to both Jews and Greeks of repentance toward God and faith in our Lord Jesus Christ." It is instructive to notice the order: repentance comes first, then faith.

Robert Sandeman argued that repentance would become part of the Christian's life after believing the gospel, but Sandeman insisted that to insist on repentance as a part of the saving transaction is wrong. Inspired Scriptures indicate that the apostle Paul made repentance a part of the gospel command, and therefore, essential to salvation. Again, Paul in his defense before King Agrippa gave the essence of his gospel. Paul said that he proclaimed "both to those of Damascus first, and also at Jerusalem and then throughout all the region of Judea, and even to the Gentiles, that they should repent and turn to God, performing deeds appropriate to repentance" (Acts 26:20). Here repentance and faith (turning to God) are linked. Repentance is not only part of our duty; it is a primary part, listed first in order. In 2 Peter 3:9, the inspired apostle wrote, "The Lord is not slow about His promise, as some count slowness, but is patient toward you, not wishing for any to perish but for all to come to repentance."

I conclude that in the preaching of the apostles, both before and after Pentecost, repentance was included as a part of the gospel.

What Is Repentance?

The Greek word *metanoia* means a change of mind. This does not exclude the emotions. Mind, emotions, and will are all inter-related in the human makeup. It is impossible to repent intellectually without also being moved at the emotional level. This is not to say that the emotions are predictable and that all respond emotionally the same way. Yet repentance is more than an intellectual exercise by which one accepts certain things as true. Indeed the gospel proclaims that the God of heaven became incarnate in the Person of Jesus Christ and died for our sins, *my* sins—that He endured the wrath of God for me, and that without Christ I am doomed to an eternity in a place called hell. If that really grips my mind, it will also grip my emotions. It is impossible not to be moved emotionally!

What then does this repentance or change of mind involve? First of all, it involves a *change of mind about sin*. The person who repents of sin sees sin as exceedingly sinful. That person, furthermore, understands that sin is against God. David prayed, "Against Thee, Thee only, I have sinned,/And done what is evil in Thy sight" (Ps. 51:4). This recognizes sin for what it is: an offense before a holy God. In repentance, one takes the perspective of God on sin and begins to have God's hatred for sin. To repent, furthermore, means that one commits to putting sin away from his or her life. The desire of the repentant sinner is to be pure and holy, like Jesus.

As the poet wrote,

Tis not enough to say, "I'm sorry," and repent,

And then go on from day to day just as I always went.

Repentance is to leave the sins we loved before,

And show that we in earnest grieve by doing them no more.

Not only is repentance a change of mind about sin, but it is a *change of mind* about God. To the unrepentant sinner God is seen either as a distant, albeit benevolent, figure; or perhaps a big bully or policeman in the sky. The Holy Spirit changes one's perception of God. The repentant sinner sees God as holy as well as loving. He is a God of justice as well as mercy. Hell is an awesome reality; as the writer of Hebrews put it, "It is a fearful thing to fall into the hands of the living God" (10:31, KJV).

Also repentance involves a change of mind about self. Pride seems to be the center and the heart of sin. Apart from the conviction of the Holy Spirit no one feels lost or undone. When the Holy Spirit does His work of conviction there is a godly sorrow for sin. One perceives himself or herself to be without Christ and without hope, spiritually bankrupt, or in the terms of Jesus, "poor in spirit" (Matt. 5:3). The result is mourning for sin (Matt. 5:4).

One who fully understands the cross of Christ and the wrath of God cannot but feel condemnation before God, and thus, will have a sorrow for sin.

What has been outlined here has been the uniform teaching of evangelical orthodoxy through the centuries. The sixteenth-century reformer John Calvin taught that repentance involves a "radical change in the repenter."[6] Both the Arminian John Wesley and Calvinist George Whitefield preached that repentance is essential to salvation. Charles Spurgeon, one of the greatest soul-winning preachers of the nineteenth century, preached as follows:

It is absolutely necessary that men should be convinced of sin. The fashionable theology is—"Convince men of the goodness of God: show them the universal fatherhood and assure them of unlimited mercy. . . ." The Holy Ghost does not come to make sinners comfortable in their sins, but to cause them to grieve over their sins. He does not help them to forget their sin, or think little of it, but He comes to con-

vince them of the horrible enormity of their iniquity. . . .
This work is most necessary, because without it there is no
leading men to receive the gospel of the grace of God.[7]

Spurgeon preached that it is easy for some to admit the facts
of the gospel, even that they are sinners, in a glib and shallow
kind of way. This admission is a mockery, however, until persons are convinced in their souls that they are sinners. When one
mourns for sin in "his inmost soul" then, "in such a man you
will find one who will welcome the gospel, welcome grace, and
welcome a Saviour."[8]

It is inconceivable that we offer the gospel of Christ to people
who are unwilling to repent. Christ came to save His people
from their sins, not *in* their sins (Matt. 1:21). John MacArthur, Jr.
said it well:

> Much of contemporary evangelism is woefully deficient
> in confronting people with the reality of their sin. Preach-
> ers offer people happiness, joy, fulfillment, and all things
> positive. Present-day Christians are taught that all they
> have to do is find a person's psychological needs, then of-
> fer Jesus as a panacea for whatever the problem is. It is
> very easy to get a response because people are looking for
> quick solutions to their felt needs. But if that's all we do, it
> is not legitimate evangelism.[9]

Repentance is a gift of the Holy Spirit (Acts 5:31; Rom. 2:4; 2
Tim. 2:25). *Real* repentance is not just a glib admission that "I'm
a sinner, sure. Everybody is a sinner. We all do wrong." Rather,
repentance is realizing that we stand before Holy God accused
and condemned of high treason, rebellion, and waywardness.
Most importantly, we must recognize that the cross stands as a
divine testimony to the sinfulness of the human heart, as well as
a testimony to the grace and love of God. When God's Spirit has
so convicted us of sin that we understand our sin and God's
grace in Christ's death, then we are prepared for a faith commitment to Christ, believing on Him unto the salvation of our souls.
Unless repentance has occurred, faith is a cold, intellectual act

which may titillate the mind but will not transform the soul. Whoever repents and believes becomes a new creature in Christ by the Holy Spirit. "It is a flat impossibility," wrote R. C. Sproul, "to be born of the Spirit and have no change in one's life. A Christian with no fruit is simply not a Christian."[10]

Is repentance a part of the gospel? You bet it is!

1. J. Gresham Machen, *Christianity and Liberalism* (Grand Rapids: Wm. B. Eerdmans Publishing Co., 1923), 105-06.

2. Charles W. Colson, *Loving God* (Grand Rapids: Zondervan Publishing House, 1983), 95.

3. Charles C. Ryrie, *So Great Salvation* (Wheaton: Victor Books, 1989), 40.

4. Ibid., 41.

5. D. Martyn Lloyd-Jones, *The Puritans: Their Origins and Successors* (Carlisle, Pa.: The Banner of Truth Trust, 1987), 170-90.

6. Timothy George, *Theology of the Reformers* (Nashville: Broadman Press, 1988), 226.

7. C. H. Spurgeon, *The Metropolitan Tabernacle Pulpit,* vol. 29 (Pasadena, Tex.: Pilgrim Publications, 1973), 125-26.

8. Ibid.

9. John F. MacArthur, Jr., *The Gospel According to Jesus* (Grand Rapids: Zondervan Publishing House), 83.

10. R. C. Sproul, *Pleasing God* (Wheaton: Tyndale House Publishers, Inc., 1988), 153.

Who Is a Disciple?

In the Christian sense then, a disciple is a person who has accepted Jesus Christ as his Lord and Savior and is seeking to learn from, obey, and follow after him as the Master of his life.

—Paul W. Powell[1]

With this in mind, it is the greatest mistake to water down the cost of Christian discipleship, or to present the church as a club where the degree of commitment depends entirely on personal choice or convenience. The church is not a club; it is the army of Jesus Christ.

—David Watson[2]

3 Who Is a Disciple?

Jesus made strong demands of those who would be His disciples. This is a problem for those who teach an easy-believism gospel, emphasizing the intellectual aspect of faith but rejecting the demand for repentance.

Jesus discussed Christian discipleship in these solemn words: "He who does not take his cross and follow after Me is not worthy of Me. He who has found his life shall lose it, and he who has lost his life for My sake shall find it" (Matt. 10:38-39).

Jesus later said, "If anyone wishes to come after Me, let him deny himself, and take up his cross, and follow Me" (Matt. 16:24). Our Lord Jesus warns would-be disciples to count the cost. "Whoever does not carry his own cross and come after Me cannot be My disciple. For which one of you, when he wants to build a tower, does not first sit down and calculate the cost, to see if he has enough to complete it?" (Luke 14:27-30). The implication is obvious. One must count the cost before building a tower, and one must count the cost involved in being a disciple and not enter lightly into this decision. Our Lord concluded, "So therefore, no one of you can be My disciple who does not give up all his own possessions" (v. 33).

Discipleship then involves total commitment.

Jesus said, "If you abide in My word, *then* you are truly disciples of Mine" (John 8:31). Elsewhere he said, "By this is My Father glorified, that you bear much fruit, and so prove to be My disciples" (John 15:8).

Discipleship involves self-denial, mortification of sin, submission to the mastery of Christ, abiding in the Word, and bearing fruit. Indeed, the disciple counts everything as nothing in order to win Christ.

In reality, however, multitudes with no intention of turning their lives over to Christ claim they believe in Him. According to the gospel of easy believism, they can be saved without a total commitment. Indeed, to require commitment would be to corrupt the gospel. "Only believe" is their slogan.

How do advocates of easy believism deal with the obvious teaching of Jesus about discipleship? If persons believe but do not reject their previous life-styles, do not forsake their sins, do not read the Bible, and do not die to self, does that mean that they are not saved? No, say advocates of easy believism. These persons are saved but are not yet disciples. They argue that disciples are a special kind of believers. They are the rare breed who have gone beyond trust in Christ and have begun obeying Christ. Disciples, by this definition, are not common believers; they are a special class of believers, those who dare to take Jesus seriously.

Zane Hodges wrote, "It is an interpretative mistake of the first magnitude to confuse the terms of discipleship with the offer of eternal life as a free gift."[3] In other words, Christ issues two calls: one to receive salvation and the other to a deeper walk called "discipleship." *Mere believers* may cling to old habits and may never totally commit to Christ. *Disciples*, on the other hand, really count the cost of following Jesus and, unlike mere believers, forsake all to do so. Hodges warned that to confuse these two levels of Christian living is to play into the hands of the enemy and to distort the Gospel.[4]

The essence of the gospel rides on this question of discipleship. Hodges himself admitted that "discipleship entailed a costly commitment."[5] On that we agree. The point of disagreement is: Are all believers also disciples? I insist that they are. The best way to settle the issue is to determine how the New Testament uses the term *disciple*. We begin with a definition: a disciple is a learner. This implies that a disciple is a follower of a teacher. This was not an exclusively Christian term at the time of Jesus, for there were many teachers who had disciples.

Unfortunately, however, this definition settles nothing. Let us go farther and ask how the New Testament uses the word. First of all, the original twelve (and then the eleven) were referred to as "disciples" (Matt. 10:1, and elsewhere). Most references to disciples in the Gospels refer to these twelve. However, Luke 19:37 speaks of "the whole multitude of the disciples," indicating that a larger group was then counted among the followers of Jesus. So the original twelve became a great multitude. In the Great Commission, Jesus commanded His followers to "make disciples." The Greek verb *matheteuo* is based on the same root as the noun *mathetes* (disciple).

Jesus' resurrection command to the church was not to make "mere believers" who intellectually embrace the gospel without a commitment of life to Christ. Rather, He commanded His church "to disciple" the nations. In other words, the only call Christ gives to a lost world is the call to discipleship.

When we look into the early church as recorded in the Book of Acts, it becomes clearer that the word *disciple* refers to all Christians. In Acts 6:1 we read that "the disciples were increasing in number." The context indicates that this refers to believers. In Acts 11:26 we read, "The disciples were first called Christians in Antioch." Here again, *disciple* equals *believer* equals *Christian*. A quick glance at a concordance will settle this issue without debate. In the Book of Acts a disciple is a believer, and all believers are called disciples. Period!

This is no word game: the very nature of the gospel is at stake. It is my contention that the advocates of easy believism have created a special class of super Christians (called disciples) in order to justify and explain the host of nominal Christians whose names decorate the rolls of churches but whose hearts have never yielded to Christ.

There is no debate that discipleship involves costly commitment. Hodges admitted that much. Yet he would have us believe that one can be born again without becoming a disciple. This is dangerous teaching. To be sure, no Christian will be perfect. Following Jesus requires a commitment, a radical break with the past. The bane of contemporary Christianity is nominal Christians who never think of yielding themselves totally to Christ. They want a ticket to heaven, not a new heart. They want happiness, not holiness. They want the grace of God with no strings attached. Let us remember Bonhoeffer's stinging words about cheap grace: "Cheap grace is grace without discipleship, grace without the cross, grace without Jesus Christ, living and incarnate."[6]

What we need to say to our generation is that not everyone who calls Jesus Savior and Lord will be saved, but only those who are seeking to do His will (Matt. 7:21). Intellectual assent to the facts of the gospel is not enough. The demons believe and shudder (Ja. 2:19). Salvation comes to those who not only believe but who repent of their sins and take up their cross and follow Jesus.

The call to be a disciple and the call to be a Christian are one and the same.

1. Paul W. Powell, *Dynamic Discipleship* (Nashville: Broadman Press, 1984), 13.

2. David Watson, *I Believe in the Church* (Grand Rapids: Wm. B. Eerdmans Publishing Co., 1978), 60.

3. Zane C. Hodges, *The Gospel Under Siege* (Dallas: Redención Viva, 1981), 37.

4. Ibid., 45.

5. Ibid., 35.

6. Dietrich Bonhoeffer, *The Cost of Discipleship* (New York: Macmillan Co., Inc., 1963), 47.

The Lordship of Christ

The preaching which is to produce conviction in the minds of men concerning their need must be that which presents the Lordship of Christ. It was the fact of the absolute supremacy of Jesus, that produced in the minds of these men the sense of their own sin. We are often being told that men to-day lack the sense of sin that characterized the thinking and conviction of our fathers. That is probably true. One of the greatest difficulties of the hour is that men are not conscious of sin. Among the reasons for this may be the fact that we have too often brought men to the Mosaic Law, and too little to the pure majesty and lonely splendour of the Lordship of Christ. There are men to-day who never tremble though they recite the Decalogue with great regularity; but we have yet to meet the man who can be brought face to face with the Lord Jesus Christ as He is presented to us in these Gospel stories, who can stand in the presence of His inherent Lordship, and of that Lordship which He won by the process of His work of redemption, without coming to the conviction of sin.

—G. Campbell Morgan[1]

To be a Christian is to have Christ as one's Lord, and thereby be freed from all other lords and powers.

—Anders Nygren[2]

4 The Lordship of Christ

I was driving to the hospital and tuned in to my favorite Christian radio station. The preaching was good, very good. The sermon had to do with commitment to Jesus Christ. Everything the preacher said was sound doctrine, and it was winsomely presented. Then he made a statement that has become all too common in these days: "Many of you have accepted Jesus as your Savior, but you have never made Him Lord of your life. That is the reason why you still have so much sin in your life. Will you not make Him your Lord today?"

As I pondered that statement, a series of questions formed in my mind. Is it possible to accept Christ as Savior and not as Lord? Is there any place in the New Testament where this is taught? If we can be saved without committing to Christ's lordship, how much of a commitment must we make in order for Christ to save us? Will Christ save those who refuse to accept His control of their lives? And what is the meaning of Christ's lordship?

Back in my study, I made some interesting discoveries. First of all, nowhere in the New Testament are we told to make Christ our Lord. Peter said that God the Father had made Him to be

Lord (Acts 2:36). Paul contended that it destiny of every human being one day is to bow before Christ and to confess that He is Lord (Phil. 2:9-11). The idea that we can "make Jesus Lord" is simply not a New Testament idea. He *is* the Lord! He claims lordship in all its prerogatives. Although that lordship is not apparent to all because the unregenerate have blinded eyes and hardened hearts, one day even they will understand it and humbly confess that He is the Lord. For them, of course, it will be too late.

You can search the New Testament, but you will never find any place where you are told you can accept Jesus as Savior and later accept Him as Lord. In fact, the terms "accept Christ" and "let Jesus come into your heart" are not biblical terms at all. In response to the jailer's query about how to be saved, Paul said, "Believe in the *Lord* Jesus, and you shall be saved" (Acts 16:31, author's italics).

In the most definitive analysis of salvation in all the Bible, Paul explained how one can be saved. "If you confess with your mouth Jesus as Lord, and believe in your heart that God raised Him from the dead, you shall be saved" (Rom. 10:9). In the very first sermon after the resurrection of our Lord, Peter preached the lordship of Christ. "Therefore let all the house of Israel know for certain that God has made Him both Lord and Christ—this Jesus whom you crucified" (Acts 2:36).

A surprising discovery awaits the one who will open the New Testament. Christ's lordship was preached to the lost. They were told to confess His lordship in order to be saved. Lordship was not something to work up to in stages—first accepting Christ as Savior, and then later acknowledging Him or making Him Lord. A Christian in the New Testament was one who was willing to confess Jesus as Lord. This was not merely a shallow verbal confession, because from the heart one must truly believe that God has raised Him from the dead, implying that in this resurrection Christ had been marked out as the Son of God and designated as Lord (Rom. 1:4).

What does the term *lord* designate? Theologian William Hendricks gave this explanation.

As a designation for Jesus, the term Lord involves: (1) a recognition of His messiahship by God's appointment; (2) an awareness of His resurrection and exaltation; (3) His particular and peculiar relationship to God to whom alone the title was appropriate in an absolute sense; (4) a particular relationship to believers expressed in the Lord (kurios)/servant (doulos) motif of Paul; (5) an affinity of lordship and glory not only in the present exaltation but also in relation to the future status; (6) an overarching term of Christians for God appropriate to Father, Son, and Spirit and, in relation to this, a sometimes ambiguous use of Lord in which it is difficult to discern whether the Father or the Son is intended (for example, 2 Tim. 1:16,18; Eph. 6:1; 1 Pet. 1:25.); (7) the confession of Jesus as Lord as an essential part of what it means to be a Christian (Rom. 10:9-10).[3]

Most New Testament scholars agree that the confession of Christ's lordship was seen as an essential part of becoming a Christian in the early days of the church. The person who would not confess "Jesus is Lord" was not regarded as a true believer. The apostle Paul seems to have taught that the whole salvation experience hinges on one's willingness to confess that Jesus is Lord (Rom. 10:9).

How then can it be said today that it is possible to accept Christ as Savior without confessing Him and recognizing Him as Lord? If lordship is essential to Christ's saviorhood, is it possible for one to be saved without acknowledging His lordship? And what is involved in the confession of Christ's lordship?

Charles Ryrie and Zane Hodges both taught that the confession of Christ's lordship only involved an acknowledgment of His deity, not His mastery over our personal lives. Commenting on Romans 10:9, Ryrie wrote that this is "the confession of Jesus as God and thus faith in the God-Man that saves from sin."[4] Ryrie suggested that it is wrong to teach that confessing Jesus as Lord means commitment to Him as Master or Sovereign. He further believed that "one can recognize the deity of

Jesus without being willing to admit His sovereignty over a particular matter."[5]   Ryrie was concerned that the standard for Christian commitment not be set too high because "if only committed people are saved people, then where is there room for carnal Christians?"[6]   That is a good question. (I will address the issue of carnal Christians in the next chapter.)

In another place Ryrie was even more blunt. "Saved people need to be dedicated, but dedication is not a requirement for being saved. Neither is willingness to be dedicated an issue in salvation."[7]

Ryrie is consistent in his teaching. He believes that salvation is a simple matter of acknowledging Jesus as having died for our sins and being raised the third day. No repentance is required. Ryrie also believes that not all believers are disciples but that discipleship is a second or third stage in Christian maturity. He consequently holds that one may be saved without submitting to Christ's lordship.

Zane Hodges is equally confident that one does not need to commit to Christ's lordship in order to be saved. Commenting on the experience of the Samaritan woman in John 4, Hodges wrote:

> It must be emphasized that there is no call here for surrender, submission, acknowledgement of Christ's lordship, or anything else of this kind. A gift is being offered to one totally unworthy of God's favor. And to get it, the woman is required to make no spiritual commitment whatsoever. She is merely invited to ask. It is precisely this impressive fact that distinguishes the true Gospel from all its counterfeits.[8]

Since comment has been made on this passage before, we will not respond to it at length. Simply note, however, that Christ confronted the woman with her sins. It was apparent that she repented and embraced His offer of salvation. She acknowledged Him as the Messiah and as her Lord.

Does the confession of Jesus' lordship (a requirement for salvation that comes only as a result of the work of the Holy Spirit,

1 Cor. 12:3) mean merely a belief in His deity? Or, does it involve a commitment to His mastery? That is the issue.

First of all, let us notice Jesus' own concept of His lordship. Wolfhart Pannenberg said, "The pre-Easter Jesus did not proclaim His own lordship."[9] The New Testament teaches otherwise. Jesus certainly proclaimed His lordship. Near the conclusion of the Sermon on the Mount, our Lord warned:

> Not everyone who says to Me, "Lord, Lord," will enter the kingdom of heaven; but he who does the will of My Father who is in heaven. Many will say to Me on that day, "Lord, Lord, did we not prophesy in Your name, and in Your name cast out demons, and in Your name perform many miracles?" And then I will declare to them, "I never knew you; depart from Me, you who practice lawlessness" (Matt. 7:21-23).

Jesus spoke of Himself as Lord and pictured Himself as being absolute sovereign over the destinies of human beings. His lordship is not a matter of His mere deity but also of His sovereignty and His judgeship. He will determine our destinies at the Judgment. In the words of our Lord, lordship is not a mere matter of acknowledging His deity but doing His will (v. 21). Lordship involves mastery or commitment.

In John 13:13-14, Jesus said to His disciples, "You call Me Teacher and Lord; and you are right, for so I am. If I then, the Lord and the Teacher, washed your feet, you also ought to wash one another's feet." In this text *Lord* does not mean merely God, it means Master or Sovereign.

Oscar Cullmann has suggested that the terms *Lord* (*kyrios*) and *king* (*basileus*) are virtually synonymous in referring to Jesus, and both indicate His sovereignty.[10] If Cullmann is right, this further strengthens the notion that in the new Testament *lord* refers to Christ's sovereignty or mastery, not merely to His deity. Confession of Christ's lordship, then, would entail confession of His control over the life of the one making the confession.

What about Romans 10:9? Is Paul teaching here that saving confession involves only the acknowledgment of Christ's deity?

Or does it also involve Christ's mastery?

Few writers have captured the thought and personality of the apostle Paul as has the brilliant James S. Stewart in *A Man in Christ*. Stewart believed that Paul's usage of the title "Lord" was deeper than a mere reference to His Messiahship or deity.

> Indeed, it would be true to say that for him it had ceased to be a title. It had become the most sacred expression of a personal devotion stronger than death. Love and gratitude and loyalty were in it. . . . No demand that Jesus could make would be too great. Life's crowning joy would be to toil unceasingly for the One who had saved him from death and from something worse than death. With glad heart Paul acknowledged himself a bondman to the greatest of all masters. He was the slave: Jesus was the Lord."[11]

For Stewart, *lord* denoted sovereign or Master even before it denoted God. In the thinking of Paul, Stewart claimed, *Kyrios* and *Doulos* are correlatives. To say "Jesus is Lord" is to say, "I am His slave."

In Thomas's wonderful confession to Christ, "My Lord and my God!" it is clear that Lord cannot mean God. It would be meaningless for Thomas to say, "My God and my God." *Lord* here must mean "Master" or ruler (John 20:28).

Reformed theologian Charles Hodge gave this insight into the meaning of Romans 10:9:

> The thing to be confessed is that Jesus Christ is Lord. That is, we must openly recognize his authority to the full extent in which he is Lord; acknowledge that he is exalted above all principality and powers, that angels are made subject to him, that all power in heaven and earth is committed unto him, and of course that he is our Lord . This confession, therefore, includes in it an acknowledgment of Christ's universal sovereignty, and a sincere recognition of his authority over us.[12]

Contemporary scholar-pastor Ray C. Stedman has also written convincingly on the meaning of Romans 10:9.

It means we have come to the place where we recognize that Jesus has the right to lordship in our lives. Up to this point we have been lord of our lives. We have run our own affairs, feeling we have the right to make our own decisions according to what we want. But there comes a time, as God's Spirit works in us and we see the reality of life as God has made it to be, that we realize that Jesus is Lord. He is Lord of our past, to forgive us our sins; he is Lord of our present, to dwell within us and to guide, direct, and control every area of our life; he is Lord of our future, to lead us into glory at last. Christ is Lord of life, Lord of death—he is Lord over all things.[13]

Someone may fear that preaching such a strong gospel may have a deleterious effect upon evangelism. On the contrary, it will sharpen our evangelism and our evangelistic efforts will become pure. Instead of offering people a truncated gospel—believe only in the Christ who will accept you just as you are without repentance—we will offer them a Christ who will change them, transform them, and become their present Lord and King.

Charles Haddon Spurgeon, one of the greatest soul-winning preachers who ever lived, was not afraid to preach a gospel of the lordship of Christ. He preached that:

Every true Christian pronounces this phrase, "Jesus our Lord," with the emphasis of unreservedness. We desire that Christ Jesus should be our Lord in everything, and Lord over every part of our being. Each one of us has said to him, "My Lord, do just what thou wilt with me." . . . Are you keeping back from him any of your substance; do you reckon that aught that you have is your own? If so, you are not true to Jesus your Lord, for he who truly loves Jesus, and who knows that he is one of those who are redeemed by him, says with all his heart that Jesus is his Lord, his absolute Sovereign, his Despot, if that word be used in the sense of Christ having unlimited monarchy and supreme sway over the soul. Yea, O "Jesus our Lord," thou shalt be the autocratic, imperial Master of our heart, and of the whole dominion of our manhood!"[14]

A little closer to our time, Southern Baptist theologian, pastor, and professor, B. H. Carroll spoke these words:

Then what is involved in being a Christian? This much is involved, that there be an absolute surrender to Jesus Christ. I mean that you recognize Him as Lord of person and of time and of property, of everything. And if He is God, He is entitled to it. If He is not God, He is a usurper and an impostor to demand anything at your hands. This is where we fail. We do play at things. People play at being Christians. They are always knowing and never able to come to the knowledge of the truth. They are always splitting hairs and caviling and discussing this little boundary, when the heart of the question is one question: Do you yield yourself and all that you have to the Lord Jesus Christ?

I do not care on what comes the issue; it may come upon a yard of ribbon. It may come upon a silver thimble. It may come upon the most infinitesimally small thing in which the human mind can take interest, but if the point on which the controversy arises be as narrow in its boundaries as the point of a cambric needle, and on that thing, however small, a soul says, "God, here you are not supreme," that is a lost soul. That is the whole of the question and it is all involved. . . .

And you might just as well write on and engage your room in hell if you deny the jurisdiction of Jesus Christ over your money, over your time, over everything.[15]

The implications of this truth for evangelism are tremendous. We must not continue calling for shallow decisions from people who have no idea who Jesus is, or who have no willingness to commit themselves to His lordship. It will also help us to clean up our evangelistic vocabulary. Instead of telling people to "invite Jesus to come into your heart" (which is unbiblical terminology), we will ask them if they are willing to acknowledge that Jesus is Lord of their lives. Or, as Ray Stedman put it:

It is helpful to see that nowhere in all the Scriptures are men ever asked to believe in Jesus as Savior. They are asked to believe in him as Lord. When you believe in him as Lord, he becomes your Savior. But you don't accept Christ as a Savior—you accept him as Lord, as the one who is in charge of all things, including you. When you come to that point, when you respond with the whole man, then God says the work of redemption is done. The miracle occurs.[16]

If Hodge, Stedman, Spurgeon, and Carroll are right (and I believe they are) then our evangelistic techniques and messages must take on a new depth. We must not only call others to accept Jesus as the Savior, we must call them to trust Jesus as their Lord and to serve Him as their King. We must challenge them to repent of their sins. Real evangelism has not occurred until men and women are confronted with their sinfulness and with Christ's finished work on the cross and His claim upon their lives as Savior and Lord.[17]

1. G. Campbell Morgan, *The Acts of the Apostles* (New York: Fleming H. Revell Co., 1924), 88.

2. Anders Nygren, *Commentary on Romans* (Philadelphia: Fortress Press, 1949), 383.

3. William L. Hendricks, *Who Is Jesus Christ?* (Nashville: Broadman Press, 1985), 126-27.

4. Charles C. Ryrie, *Balancing the Christian Life* (Chicago: Moody Press, 1969), 175.

5. Ibid., 174.

6. Ibid., 170.

7. Charles C. Ryrie, *So Great Salvation* (Wheaton: Victor Books, 1989), 74.

8. Zane C. Hodges, *The Gospel Under Siege* (Dallas: Redención Viva, 1981), 14.

9. Wolfhart Pannenberg, *Jesus—God and Man* (Philadelphia: The Westminster Press. 1968), 365.

10. Oscar Cullman, *The Christology of the New Testament* (Philadelphia: The Westminster Press, 1959), 220-21.

11. James S. Stewart, *A Man in Christ* (Grand Rapids: Baker Book House, 1975), 302.

12. Charles Hodge, *Commentary on the Epistle to the Romans* (Grand Rapids: Wm. B. Eerdmans Publishing Co., 1950), 341.

13. Ray C. Stedman, *Expository Studies in Romans 9:16: From Guilt to Glory,* vol. 2 (Waco: Word, Inc., 1978), 42.

14. C. H. Spurgeon, *Expository Encyclopedia,* vol. 3 (Grand Rapids: Baker Book House, 1984), 192.

15. B. H. Carroll, *Jesus the Christ* (Nashville: The Broadman Press, 1937), 162-63, 166.

16. Stedman, *Expository Studies,* 43-44.

17. See J. I. Packer, *Evangelism and the Sovereignty of God* (Downers Grove, Ill.: Inter-Varsity Press, 1961), 39-40.

What About Carnal Christians?

Sanctification, then, is the invariable result of that vital union with Christ which true faith gives to a Christian.—"He that abideth in Me, and I in him, the same bringeth forth much fruit." (John xv.5.) The branch which bears no fruit is no living branch of the vine. The union with Christ which produces no effect on heart and life is a mere formal union, which is worthless before God. The faith which has not a sanctifying influence on the character is no better than the faith of devils. It is a "dead faith, because it is alone." It is not the gift of God. It is not the faith of God's elect. In short, where there is no sanctification of life, there is no real faith in Christ.

—J. C. Ryle[1]

When the Holy Spirit comes into our lives at our salvation, he comes to make us holy in practice. If there is not, then, at least a yearning in our hearts to live a holy life pleasing to God, we need to seriously question whether our faith in Christ is genuine.

—Jerry Bridges[2]

In a panic over this phenomenon, the evangelicals have invented the idea of 'carnal Christians.' These are said to be folks who have taken the gift of eternal life without turning from sin. They have 'allowed' Jesus to be their Saviour; but they have not yet yielded their life to the Lord. Trying to patch up a faulty evangelism, the church has adopted a faulty follow-up. . . .

Needless to say, the Bible knows of no such grotesque creature as one who is saved but unrepentant.

—Walter J. Chantry[3]

5 What About Carnal Christians?

One critic of the view taken in this book has said, "If only committed people are saved people, then where is there room for carnal Christians?"[4]

That question goes to the heart of the issue. If salvation means a repentance from sin and a commitment to the lordship of Jesus Christ and a counting the cost in becoming a disciple, then what about those who have made a decision for Christ and intellectually believed, yet, have never done those things just described? They are not disciples; they are not committed to Christ's lordship, and they have never really repented of their sinful lifestyles. Are these carnal Christians? Are they babes who have been born and yet have never grown? Or is it possible that many people who are called carnal Christians are not Christians at all? Obviously, this is a question of tremendous importance.

When I was a teenager going to church in a small town in Louisiana, I could predict that several things would happen every Sunday in our worship service. I knew that the song service would last about twenty minutes. I knew that the preacher would preach about thirty minutes, and that he would be through before twelve o'clock. I also knew, just about as predictable as clockwork, that Brenda Smith (not her real name) would walk the aisle nearly every Sunday to rededicate her life to Christ. We teenagers knew why Brenda felt she needed to frequently rededicate her life. Her character was well known around campus. She rededicated her life nearly every Sunday because her life-style and her profession were contradictions. This went on for several years until, finally, Brenda became pregnant and married a young man who supposedly was the father of her child. Brenda also used alcohol to excess and had a foul mouth.

Now what can be said about Brenda? One view is that, since she had made a profession of faith, she was saved but still a babe in Christ—a carnal Christian. She just needed to grow. Another view is that Brenda was a lost church member who trifled with Christian commitment. She believed the gospel intellectually but had never given her life to Jesus Christ.

Because there are so many professing Christians whose lives are morally out of harmony with the biblical picture of a Christian, some acknowledge a class of carnal Christians. Perhaps the first theologian to do so was Lewis Sperry Chafer in his 1918 publication entitled *He that Is Spiritual*. In the first chapter, Chafer distinguished what he called "three classes of men": the *natural* man, the lost person who does not know Christ; the *carnal* man, shown by the Christian whose spiritual walk is no different than a lost person's; and the *spiritual* man, who is a Christian walking in fellowship with the Lord and in the power of the indwelling Spirit.

Chafer's view was a novelty at the time and opposed by leading biblical scholars, but it has since become commonplace to speak of "carnal Christians." Few evangelicals would even suspect that this is not a biblical concept. Then the other view that being a Christian involves a commitment to the lordship of Jesus Christ seems provincial, narrow, and uncourteous.

What some call a carnal Christian looks a lot like what the Bible describes as a lost person. Evangelist Billy Sunday said, "You might as well talk about a heavenly devil as a worldly Christian." The Bible nowhere teaches that a person can believe on Jesus Christ and genuinely be saved without a transformed life.

Let's look at Paul's teaching on this subject:

I, brethren, could not speak to you as to spiritual men, but as to men of flesh, as to babes in Christ. I gave you milk to drink, not solid food; for you were not yet able to receive it. Indeed, even now you are not yet able, for you are still fleshly. For since there is jealousy and strife among you, are you not fleshly, and are you not walking like mere men?" (1 Cor. 3:1-3.)

Now Corinth was far from perfect. The Corinthians were divided over preachers (chapter 3). One member was cohabiting with his stepmother (chapter 5). Some church members had taken other church members to court (chapter 6). There was disagreement over the place of sex in marriage (chapter 7) and dispute about meat offered to idols (chapter 8). Some members were making gluttons of themselves at the agape feast (chapter 11). This church was obviously struggling with the surrounding culture, seeking to implement the ethic and moral demands of Jesus Christ.

There was carnality among some of the members; some were giving in to the temptation of the flesh and compromising their Christian commitment. The church as a whole was perhaps not so mature as other churches. The oldest Christians were just a few years old in the Lord, and one would not expect this congregation to be as mature as the Antioch church. Even so, in calling the congregation "babes" or "men of flesh," Paul was not creating a category of carnal Christians. He did not intend to leave the impression that some are saved but retain carnality, continuing to walk as though they have never received the Spirit of Christ. Paul admitted that there was carnality in some aspects of the church's life and of the members' lives. This does not mean, however, that there was such a thing as a "carnal Christian."

Perhaps Benjamin B. Warfield summed it up in his review of Chafer's book in 1919:

The remainders of the flesh in the Christian do not constitute his characteristic. He is in the Spirit and is walking, with however halting steps, by the Spirit; and it is to all Christians, not to some, that the great promise is given, "Sin shall not have dominion over you," and the great assurance is added, "Because you are not under the law but under grace." He who believes in Jesus Christ is under grace, and his whole course, in its process and in its issue alike, is determined by grace, and therefore, having been predestined to be conformed to the image of God's Son, he is surely being conformed to that image, God Himself seeing to it that he is not only called and justified but also glorified. You may find Christians at every stage of this process, for it is a process through which all must pass; but you will find none who will not in God's own good time and way pass through every stage of it. There are not two kinds of Christians, although there are Christians at every conceivable stage of advancement towards the one goal to which all are bound and at which all shall arrive.[5]

The apostle Paul did not refer to one living in overt sin as a carnal Christian, even if that one had made a profession of faith in Christ. Paul would not even call the immoral man of chapter 5 a brother. He referred to him as a "so-called brother" (v. 11), because, while the man was living in known and unconfessed sin, no obvious evidence was being given that he had been born again. It would become obvious when the man put away his sin to pursue a life of holiness. Paul called on the church to discipline the "brother" and indicated that the Lord would discipline him. The church responded (2 Cor. 2:4-11). He did repent and showed himself to be a brother. The man did not need counseling for sexual addiction; he needed loving discipline from a believing congregation. When he received this, he repented and began to walk aright.

Paul's teaching in 1 Corinthians 6 also flies in the face of the carnal Christian doctrine:

Or do you not know that the unrighteous shall not inherit the kingdom of God? Do not be deceived; neither fornicators, nor idolaters, nor adulterers, nor effeminate, nor homosexuals, nor thieves, nor the covetous, nor drunkards, nor revilers, nor swindlers, shall inherit the kingdom of God" (vv. 6:9-10).

Paul meant that those who habitually engage in these sins are not saved and will not go to heaven. We may call them carnal Christians, but Paul would call them lost people.

Then Paul continued: "And such were some of you; but you were washed, but you were sanctified, but you were justified in the name of the Lord Jesus Christ, and in the Spirit of our God" (v. 11). Paul spoke in the past tense. He didn't say, "Such *are* some of you because you're carnal Christians." Rather he said, "Such *were* some of you (author's italics). Because you met Jesus Christ, you were justified by faith, indwelled by the Spirit of God, and sanctified by that same Spirit; therefore, these things are in your past." True, a Christian may fall into sin but does not live in sin, according to the New Testament.

Writing to the Christians at Colossae, Paul said, "Therefore consider the members of your earthly body as dead to immorality, impurity, passion, evil desire, and greed, which amounts to idolatry. For it is on account of these things that the wrath of God will come, and in them you also once walked, when you were living in them" (Col. 3:5-7).

Here again, Paul wrote of the acts of the flesh as being in the past. A Christian can commit an act of immorality or passion, but Paul said categorically that Christians are not now walking or living in those carnal acts. One who walks in these deeds or lives in them is not a carnal Christian, that person is lost.

Just as explicit is Paul's teaching in Galatians 5:

"Now the deeds of the flesh are evident, which are: immorality, impurity, sensuality, idolatry, sorcery, enmities, strife, jealousy, outbursts of anger, disputes, dissensions, factions, envying, drunkenness, carousing, and things like these, of which I forewarn you just as I have forewarned you that those who practice such things shall not inherit the kingdom of God (vv. 19-21).

Language could not be plainer. A Christian does not walk in, that is, practice, such a life-style. A born-again person may fall into sin, but he or she does not live in sin. I fear that the creation of a category of "carnal Christians" has given comfort to professing Christians who are really lost church members. The high standard of biblical morality has been lowered in order to accommodate worldly members who have no intention of kneeling before Jesus Christ as their Lord.

If the saved get into sin, the Holy Spirit will convict them. If conviction alone does not bring them to repentance, then the process of discipline will begin. "For whom the Lord loveth he chasteneth" (Heb. 12:6, KJV). If temporal discipline does not work, the Lord will call the disobedient saint home in the ultimate act of spiritual excommunication (1 Cor. 11:30). There is a sin unto death, and unrepentant Christians are liable to have the Lord bring them home prematurely rather than risk damaging the reputation of Christ by living a double life (1 John 5:16).

To sum up, do Christians sin? Yes, indeed. "If we say that we have no sin, we are deceiving ourselves, and the truth is not in us" (1 John 1:8). Do Christians live in habitual sin? Not according to 1 John 3:6-9:

> No one who abides in Him sins; no one who sins has seen Him or knows Him. Little children, let no one deceive you; the one who practices righteousness is righteous, just as He is righteous; the one who practices sin is of the devil; for the devil has sinned from the beginning. The Son of God appeared for this purpose, that He might destroy the works of the devil. No one who is born of God practices sin, because His seed abides in him; and he cannot sin, because he is born of God.

S. Lewis Johnson, Jr. was right when he said, "The term *the carnal Christian*, therefore, is not a category of a Christian acceptable to God, nor does it represent a *permanent* status in the Christian life."[6] R. C. Sproul has put it plainly:

There is a widespread notion within evangelical Christianity that there are two distinctive types of Christians. There is the carnal Christian and the spiritual Christian. . . .

This distinction is fraught with peril. . . . This distortion rests upon a false view of grace and forgiveness. It includes the idea that a person can receive Christ as Savior but not as Lord. It assumes a faith without obedience, a faith with no fruit of good works. This is precisely the kind of "dead faith" of which James writes, a faith that is no faith, a faith that can never please God.

Here the carnal Christian is one who is said to believe in Christ but lives a life of consistent carnality, giving no evidence of the fruit of the Spirit. This represents a fatal contradiction in terms. Such a person may not be called a carnal Christian. He must be considered a carnal non-Christian. If a person manifests a life of pure and consistent carnality, he is no Christian. He has not the Spirit of Christ living in him. It is a flat impossibility to be born of the Spirit and have no change in one's life. A Christian with no fruit is simply not a Christian.[7]

1. J. C. Ryle, *Holiness* (Grand Rapids: Associated Publishers and Authors, 1971), 11.

2. Jerry Bridges, *The Pursuit of Holiness* (Colorado Springs: Nav Press, 1978), 38.

3. Walter J. Chantry, *Today's Gospel: Authentic or Synthetic:* (Carlisle, Pa.: Banner of Truth Trust, 1970), 54.

4. Charles C. Ryrie, *Balancing the Christian Life* (Chicago: Moody Press, 1969), 170.

5. Benjamin B. Warfield, review of *He that Is Spiritual* by Lewis S. Chafer in *The Princeton Theological Review* (April 1919, 322-27; quoted by John F. MacArthur, Jr., in *The Gospel According to Jesus* (Grand Rapids: Zondervan Publishing House, 1988), 24.

6. S. Lewis Johnson, Jr., "How Faith Works," *Christianity Today,* September 22, 1989, 25.

7. R. C. Sproul, *Pleasing God* (Wheaton: Tyndale House Publishers, Inc., 1988), 152-53.

Legalism Through the Back Door?

To make light of works because we are not justified by works, is the same thing in effect as to make light of all religion, all grace and holiness, yea, true evangelical holiness, and all gracious experience; for all is included, when the Scripture says, we are not justified by works; . . . It would be legal to suppose that holy practice justifies by bringing us to a title to Christ's benefits as the price of it, . . . but it is not legal to suppose, that holy practice justifies the sincerity of a believer, as the proper evidence of it.

—*Jonathan Edwards[1]*

The conscience of believers does not gain assurance of justification from seeking to keep the Law, but from embracing God's mercy in Christ. The Law has no legal obligation to which the conscience of believers is answerable before the tribunal of God. No longer does it stand over the believer saying "Do this and thou shalt live . . . in the hour that thou eatest thereof thou shalt surely die."

But the Law is a reminder to the Christian of his call to sanctification; it is an impetus to the fulfillment of his duties in voluntary obedience to the will of God. While believers are not justified before God by their personal obedience to the moral law, they are, as the Scottish principal, George Hill, expressed it, "as much bound to obey it as if another method of justification had not been revealed to them."

—*Carl F. H. Henry[2]*

6 Legalism Through the Back Door?

One of my favorite seminary courses was an intensive study of the Book of Romans. We came to Chapter 6, where Paul addressed the question of whether or not a Christian can continue to live in sin. The professor said that we have not preached the gospel unless people ask whether we can live as we please if the gospel is so simple. He reasoned that a faithful presentation of the simple gospel always raises the issue of libertinism.

This raised the curiosity of a student who probed him further about the relation of faith and works. If we are saved, will we produce good works? Is not holy living a result of salvation by faith? The professor paused for a moment, then responded that this kind of thinking is "legalism through the back door." Works have nothing to do with salvation, and it is not proper to predict what kind of life a believer will have. The teacher asserted that the gospel has nothing to do with legalism or works, whether those works are said to be necessary for salvation or a result of salvation.

"Legalism through the back door"—what a nice slogan. My professor's argument sounded only too good. With all due respect, however, I must disagree with him. Paul would have disagreed with him. That seems to be the burden of Romans 6.

The New Testament says a lot about our behavior. We must not dilute the messages fearing accusations of "legalism." Like my professor, Charles Ryrie and Zane Hodges argued that it is a corruption of the gospel to say that salvation will produce good works. Works are not even to be mentioned, either as a cause or a result of salvation. Ryrie even suggested that a college student could "be saved at the dorm meeting one evening and yet spend that same night in a continuing adulterous relationship." He or she might even continue that relationship for months.[3]

It is the purpose of this chapter to show that there is a place for good works in Christian thinking. The New Testament has a clear doctrine of sanctification. In traditional evangelical theology, justification always leads to sanctification. Even Lewis Sperry Chafer taught that works are *the proper test of saving faith* and that "true salvation will be manifested outwardly by good works."[4]

Before looking to the Scriptures it ought to be noted that both Luther and Calvin, with slightly differing twists, taught that good works result from justification.[5] Reformed theology since Calvin has emphasized the believer's union with Christ by which the sin nature is put to death and good works are produced as fruit. "Justification is received by faith alone, but since that faith unites us to Christ as sanctifier, justification and sanctification can no more be separated than Christ himself can be divided."[6] No one taught a higher view of grace than did John Calvin and his successors. Yet they argued consistently that justification and sanctification cannot be separated; the Christ who saves and the Christ who sanctifies is one.

The English Reformers Tyndale, Latimer, Cranmer, Becon, Sandys, Jewel, Pilkington, and others taught that good works are the outward evidence of true faith in Christ, and that if works are absent the faith is spurious. Philip E. Hughes wrote:

Holiness of life must be natural to him who has a new nature through the inward operation of the Holy Spirit: a good tree must be expected to bring forth good fruit. Sanctification, therefore, was regarded by the Reformers as essential and, inasmuch as regeneration is altogether the work of God, inevitable for the man who has been freely justified by faith in Christ Jesus."[7]

When Christ comes to live in the believer at conversion, the believer begins to manifest the character of the Lord. Imperfectly, of course, but more and more until the process is completed in what theologians call "glorification," which is but the completion of sanctification. According to Paul, God's sovereign pleasure settles this process of justification, sanctification, and glorification (Rom. 8:29-30).

Did our Lord teach that good works would characterize His followers? In the conclusion to the Sermon on the Mount, Jesus said that only those who obey the Father, not merely those who call Jesus "Lord," will enter the kingdom of heaven (Matt. 7:21-23). Jesus concluded the Sermon on the Mount with the parable of the two houses, one built upon the rock and the other built upon the sand. Jesus taught that the ultimate distinction between people is that of obedience to Christ. Disobedience leads to destruction, which in the context means exclusion from the kingdom of God. Obedience to Christ means security and entrance into the kingdom of Christ.

In John 15, Jesus presents some of the clearest New Testament teaching on sanctification. Using the analogy of the vine and the branch, the Lord Jesus teaches that it is the believer's union with Christ that assures the Christian's growth and productivity. Our Lord mentions three levels of productivity: (1) fruit, (2) more fruit, and (3) much fruit (John 15:2,8). A non-fruitbearing Christian is unthinkable. Jesus says the withered branch is "taken away." This could refer to the discipline of an early death of a nonproductive believer, or it could refer to the ultimate eternal destruction of one who bears no fruit because he or she is not united to Christ. Either way, Jesus is clearly teaching that a believer will bear fruit.

These three levels of fruitfulness correspond to Jesus' parable of the soils in Matthew 13. The good soil, which represents the true believer, receives the seed and produces thirtyfold or sixtyfold or a hundredfold. Jesus' teaching in this parable is unmistakable. Four kinds of soil represent four kinds of professing believers. Three of the soils brought forth no fruit and represented false professors who were never saved. The good soil represents one who was genuinely saved and brought forth fruit.

Jesus taught in Matthew 13 and John 15 that there are *degrees of productivity*, but all true believers bear some fruit. The passage in John 15 teaches that fruit bearing results from the believer's union with Christ. It is unthinkable, then, that one could believe in Jesus Christ, receive the indwelling Spirit, yet not be productive. Jesus expected His followers to be different, to grow, and to change. As Gary Collins put it, "Never did Jesus tell anyone to 'follow me, but stay just the way you are.'"[8]

In discussing Romans 6, Ryrie and Hodges suggested that it is wrong to mention works in discussing salvation. Why did Paul do exactly this? The Epistle to the Romans, Paul's magnum opus, includes the greatest explanation of salvation ever written. Paul hardly finished discussing justification before he began discussing sanctification, the believer's victory over sin. The apostle found it unthinkable for a Christian to live in sin after being justified by faith (Rom. 6:2). In the new birth the Christian has experienced the death of the old life and a resurrection to a new life (vv. 4-5). The believer is victorious over indwelling sin, once having been united with Christ; the old nature or self has been crucified with Christ (vv. 5-6). Therefore (v. 11), a believer should realize that he or she is dead to the power of sin and liberated to live righteously in Jesus Christ. Sin is not a necessity (v. 12), and righteousness is a possibility (v. 13). Paul concluded, "For sin shall not be master over you" (v. 14).

Nothing could be plainer. We are justified by faith (Rom. 5:1). When we are justified, the living Christ comes to live in our lives. We have the power to put to death the old life. It is, therefore, impossible for us to be mastered by sin. If we are genuinely saved, we will continually grow in righteousness. The New Testament and theologians call this growth "sanctification," or, as Paul put it, "Having been freed from sin and enslaved to God, you derive your benefit, resulting in sanctification, and the outcome, eternal life" (6:22).

Equally clear is Paul's teaching on grace in Ephesians 2:8-10. "For by grace you have been saved through faith; and that not of yourselves, it is the gift of God; not as a result of works, that no one should boast." Too many readers stop at this point—and it is a good place to pause and reflect. We are saved by grace apart from human effort; our works do not contribute to our salvation.

Salvation is totally of the Lord and a gift to be accepted by faith. There is no debating this. Yet, Paul did not stop here. He went on to consider what happens as a result of salvation: "For we are His workmanship, created in Christ Jesus for good works, which God prepared beforehand, that we should walk in them." It would seem that this could not be misunderstood, though Zane Hodges confused the obvious meaning. He said that God intended for good works to result, but he argued that the apostle did not affirm that good works will indeed be realized.[9]

Hodges' interpretation makes no sense at all. Paul was giving the Ephesian readers a panorama of salvation. In chapter 1 he began in eternity past with God's choice of the believer before the foundation of the world. In chapter 2, he pointed out that the believer contributed nothing to salvation, being dead in trespasses and sins and having nothing to offer. Even the believer's faith resulted from God's grace (v. 8). No good thing that the believer has done could merit salvation. Even the righteous life that the believer will certainly lead is a result of the grace of God (v. 10), for we are His workmanship. The believer is a new creation (recreated in Christ Jesus), and that new creation will inevitably produce "good works." These good works, like the believer's salvation itself, were "prepared beforehand;" therefore, the believer will "walk in them." This is the simple meaning of these verses.

John MacArthur, Jr., summarized his interpretation of this passage in the following way:

> We must remember above all that salvation is a sovereign work of God. Biblically it is defined by what it produces, not by what one does to get it. Works are not necessary to earn salvation. But true salvation wrought by God will not fail to produce the good works that are its fruit (cf. Matthew 7:17). We are God's workmanship. No aspect of salvation is merited by human works (Titus 3:5-7). Thus salvation cannot be defective in any dimension. As a part of His saving work, God will produce repentance, faith, sanctification, yieldedness, obedience, and ul-

timately glorification. Since He is not dependent on human effort in producing those elements, an experience that lacks any of them cannot be the saving work of God.[10]

Paul believed that our life-style indicates whether or not we are true believers. He speaks of those who "profess to know God, but by their deeds they deny Him, being detestable and disobedient, and worthless for any good deed" (Titus 1:16). The apostle is not describing a "carnal Christian" or a disobedient believer. He is describing a false professor, one who claims to know God but doesn't. Our life-styles will show whether we truly believe in Christ.

Proponents of easy believism would accuse Paul of legalism. They would say that one does not really believe in salvation by grace if he or she makes good works a test of faith. In fact, Paul believed in the grace of God, and he believed that the grace of God made a difference human lives. That is what he is talking about in Titus 2:11-12. "For the grace of God has appeared, bringing salvation to all men, instructing us to deny ungodliness and worldly desires and to live sensibly, righteously and godly in the present age."

Any teaching that magnifies a stale grace unable to produce holiness has prostituted the grace of God. In Paul's view, God's grace always brings salvation. When that salvation comes to us, it teaches us about self-denial and righteousness, not merely in the age to come but in the present. The grace of God teaches born-again believers to live Christ-honoring lives, not just "in the sweet bye and bye" but in the "nasty here and now."

Proponents of easy believism and cheap grace seem to forget that salvation is a supernatural act. It is not something that we do. God through His Spirit convicts of sin, and God through His Spirit regenerates us, creating in us a new nature. The indwelling Christ produces a character to glorify the Lord. As Paul put it in Titus 3:5, "He saved us, not on the basis of deeds which we have done in righteousness, but according to His mercy, by the washing of regeneration and renewing by the Holy Spirit."

Salvation is all of grace. It is supernatural from start to finish.

The believer offers no works in exchange for salvation. When the Spirit of God indwells a human life, He gives us a new creature. The inevitable result is fruit bearing, discipleship, repentance, and a changed life.

As I pondered my esteemed professor's pithy slogan, I concluded that there is something worse than legalism through the back door: it is libertinism through the front door. The doctrine of cheap grace has opened our churches to multitudes who profess that they know Jesus but whose deeds deny Him (Titus 1:16). Even if the case for holiness may be overstated, our ungodly age can easily stand it. It is unfair and eternally destructive to promise to the world a gift of eternal life on the basis of a shallow belief in Christ without any repentance or commitment, and it is disastrous to Christian living. This shallow preaching discourages genuine Christians, and many are discouraged from seeking "holiness without which no man shall see the Lord" (Heb. 12:14, KJV). As Bonhoeffer phrased it so succinctly, "The word of cheap grace has been the ruin of more Christians than any commandment of works."[11]

1. Jonathan Edwards, *The Works of Jonathan Edwards,* A Treatise Concerning Religious Affections, vol. 1 (Carlisle, Pa.: Banner of Truth Trust, 1834), 377-78.

2. Carl F. H. Henry, *Christian Personal Ethics* (Grand Rapids: Wm. B. Eerdmans Publishing Co., 1957), 356.

3. Charles C. Ryrie, *So Great Salvation* (Chicago: Moody Press, 1969), 49.

4. Lewis S. Chafer, *Grace* (Wheaton: Van Kampen Press, 1922), 26.

5. Timothy George, *Theology of the Reformers* (Nashville: Broadman Press, 1988), 72-73, 226.

6. Sinclair B. Ferguson, "The Reformed View," *Christian Spirituality: Five Views of Sanctification* (Downers Grove, Ill.: Inter-Varsity Press, 1988), 54.

7. Philip E. Hughes, *Theology of the English Reformers* (Grand Rapids: Wm. B. Eerdmans Publishing Co., 1965), 79.

8. Gary R. Collins, *Beyond Easy Believism* (Waco, Tex.: Word, Inc., 1982), 32.

9. Zane C. Hodges, *The Gospel Under Siege* (Dallas: Redención Viva, 1981), 16.

10. John F. MacArthur, Jr., *The Gospel According to Jesus* (Grand Rapids: Zondervan Publishing House, 1988), 33.

11. Dietrich Bonhoeffer, *The Cost of Discipleship* (New York: Macmillan Co., Inc., 1963), 59.

Assurance

God's Spirit gives this blessed confidence of sins forgiven to those who examine themselves in the light of God's Word. 'Examine yourselves whether ye be in the faith; prove your own selves'. 'If a man loves me he will keep my words: and my Father will love him, and we will come unto him, and make our abode with him'.

The promises of the Bible respecting assurance are not given indiscriminately. They never lead men to expect that they can be in a state of acceptance with God without their also being renewed in a state of holiness.

—Walter J. Chantry[1]

Dear Brethren, the Scripture teaches us in all ways that we can know indeed that we ought to have a proper certainty whether we are in grace with God or not. But this must be known according to certain indicators. It is not my meaning that one is to only firmly imagine that he is a child of God and is only to believe in a blind way that he certainly stands with God in grace, that without doubt he will be eternally blessed and that throughout everything he will not doubt concerning his blessedness, but that everything which comes into his mind he is to hold as a demonic temptation and to firmly and continually believe that he is a child of God. This notion is in no way taught by God's word but God's word teaches us with great care that we are to distinguish properly between a state of grace and a state of wrath from the indicators of both. Therefore, let each person guard himself against misuse of the doctrine and take very great care that he follow through in the testing to see whether he is a Christian or not.

—*August Hermann Francke*[2]

7 Assurance

According to the Scriptures, all believers bear spiritual fruit and demonstrate through their changed lives that they have indeed received eternal life. It is possible that "for a time" the child of God may walk in temporary disobedience; but, as Chafer says, "At such a time there will be abnormal results in his life before God and before the world."[3]

The thesis of this book is that a life of discipleship, fruit bearing, and obedience is normal for the regenerate person. In the last chapter we saw that some charge this teaching with legalism. Even more, these same teachers allege that, if we regard works as the inevitable result of saving grace, we confuse eternal security and assurance. Since "one cannot really be certain until the end of his earthly experience whether he has abided or persevered in the requisite obedience,"[4] assurance then, according to this charge, would be impossible to the believer until death, at which time he or she would have continued faithful to the end.

This is a serious charge, but—like the charge of legalism—it results from fuzzy thinking. The Bible clearly teaches that those who are truly born of God are eternally secure in Christ.

Lewis S. Chafer discussed God's twelve provisions of grace to ensure that His purposes will never fail and that the Christian will never ultimately fall. These are:

- The power of God;
- The love of God;
- The prayer of the Son of God (John 17);
- The substitutionary death of the Son of God;
- The resurrection of the Son of God;
- The present advocacy of the Son of God;
- The intercession, or shepherdhood, of the Son of God;
- The regenerating work of the Spirit;
- The Spirit's indwelling;
- The baptism with the Spirit;
- The sealing with the Spirit;
- The New Covenant made in His blood.[5]

A stronger case for security could hardly be made, and with that this writer concurs. God has determined that His purposes in grace will never fail, and He so secures the believer in Christ that the one who has been redeemed by grace can never ultimately fall. Believers will be preserved in grace; they will persevere in holiness; they will maintain that standard of good works, though now and then they may, indeed will, fall into transgression; and they will be presented at the last day as holy and complete in Christ. This is the uniform teaching of the New Testament, and it is traditional evangelical doctrine.

Many Evangelicals today confuse *security* with *assurance*. The two are not identical. Someone may *be* secure but may not *feel* secure. For instance, suppose a man is walking through the woods and comes upon a large frozen lake. He doesn't want to take the time to walk around the lake, but he isn't sure how thick the ice is. He believes the ice is thick enough to support him, but he isn't totally sure of the thickness of the ice. He begins crawling across the lake on hands and knees, inching his way ever so cautiously toward the center. Quite a ways out he begins to think that he has made a mistake. He fears that at any moment the ice may crumble and that he will be plunged into the icy waters to certain death. The thought overwhelms his mind. Then he hears a noise behind him. He turns to see another traveler walking, nearly running across the frozen ice. He seems to have not a care in the world. As he approaches, he says, "Is there a problem? Why are you down on your knees?" The first traveler says, "Well, I wanted to go across this ice to save myself a few steps, but I wasn't sure how thick it is. I decided to crawl rather than to walk." The second traveler laughs and says, "This ice is several feet thick. It would be impossible for it to crack beneath your feet. You can stand up and go on your way without any fear." So they both traveled carefree across the rest of the lake.

Now the first traveler lacked assurance for a time, but he was secure. The second was no more secure than the first, but he had a great deal more confidence or assurance.

It is possible to be secure yet not to have assurance. Many of God's children wrestle with doubts all of their lives. They *are* secure, but they never quite feel secure. They have a strong confidence in the grace of God and the provision for their sins made by Christ at Calvary, yet for many reasons these frail saints doubt their salvation. One reason, I believe, is that evangelists and pastors have confused assurance with security. They have become so concerned that many church members have a false confidence in salvation they have shaken the confidence of those who are genuinely saved. Their motives are good, but the result is disastrous; it has unsettled true believers and given false confidence to the unregenerate.

These preachers have substituted unbiblical language and unbiblical tests to determine one's salvation. These are "sacred cows," and when I mention them, many will object; however, the Word of God—not tradition—is our guide.

One unbiblical way of preaching assurance is to insist that believers must remember exactly when they were saved. According to this view, if we can remember the exact moment when we prayed the sinner's prayer, then we are saved. That settles it. Nothing else is very important so long as we remember the time.

The Bible never teaches this. If it were important for a person to remember the time when he or she was born again, then the

New Testament would say that very plainly. I personally remember the moment that I prayed and committed my life to Jesus Christ; perhaps most Christians do. Yet some Christians do not, and this is not a matter of ultimate concern.

> Charles Spurgeon encouraged his people in the following way:
> Do not I hear someone say, "I trust I am a Christian; I believe I have experienced a great change of heart; but I do not remember the time?" Beloved friend, there is an old legal maxim that "possession is nine points of the law," and as long as you have got Christ, I am not going to raise many questions about when you got him. Surely, if the hold you have be equivalent to nine points of the law, it represents all the points of the gospel. If you have got Christ, he will never be taken away from you. If you are resting upon his blood and righteousness, it is well enough; and, if you are producing the fruits of the Spirit, and your life is what it should be, by your fruits you are to be known. We shall ask you no more questions.[6]

I know that I am alive physically. How do I know that? Not because I can remember the exact moment of my birth, though I have a birth certificate that verifies the time. I do not recall it, yet the evidence is real that I am alive.

Again, the New Testament does not emphasize remembering when one prayed a prayer. The emphasis is on the kind of life being lived and the faith being expressed in the present. "The ultimate question we face is not *when* we were converted or *where* we were converted. The only real question is whether we *are* converted."[7]

When Paul spoke of justifying faith in Romans 5:1 and elsewhere, he was not referring to the initial experience of trusting Christ. Faith is the abiding attitude of confidence in the finished work of Christ on Calvary.

Someone may remember exactly when and where they voiced the sinner's prayer, but that person may not have prayed in a warm confidence in the blood of Jesus Christ to save. Another person may not remember when he or she first believed, though the person trusts totally in the finished work of the cross and in the grace of God through Christ without confidence in the flesh. Ruth Graham, wife of evangelist Billy Graham and daughter of missionary parents, cannot remember when she first believed in Christ.[8]

Others are insisting you must remember the *prayer* that you prayed in order to know that you are saved. You must have prayed the right kind of prayer. You are asked, "Did you ask Jesus to come into your heart?" (Never mind that this is an un-biblical question. Nowhere in the Scriptures are we commanded to "ask Jesus to come into our hearts.") The Bible never gives us a specific prayer for salvation. In fact, there is no record of anybody praying a specific kind of prayer by which he or she was saved.

As a pastor, I have counseled with many persons whose faith had been shaken because a preacher said that if they did not invite Jesus into their hearts He did not come in, even though they believed the gospel and were resting their salvation solely upon Christ. Although this preaching shakes some false professors, just as often true believers have their confidence in Christ's finished work temporarily shaken because they are told that they must look at themselves and their prayer rather than looking to the cross and the work of Christ.

The New Testament teaches that believers can be sure that they are saved. True believers are secure, and a secure believer can be sure. It is equally true that an unsaved person can have a false assurance. No one was more shocked than the religious professors who heard the Lord Jesus tell them, "Depart from Me, thou who practice lawlessness." They argued with the Lord because they were confident that, if anybody was saved, they were saved. Yet their assurance was false. (See Matt. 7:22-23.)

What is the New Testament teaching about assurance? How can a Christian really know that he or she has been born again? If the emphasis is not on the initial experience or on remembering the words of the prayer, how does the New Testament teach that one can have inward assurance of new life in Christ?

John wrote his first epistle for the express purpose of helping believers to assure their hearts before the Lord. "These things I have written to you who believe in the name of the Son of God, in order that you may know that you have eternal life" (5:13).

The Gnostic heresy of John's day held that only a few spiritually elite Christians were gifted with deep spiritual insight and thus would know of their security in Christ. John wrote to comfort the hearts of true believers by giving them the evidences of eternal life. This little epistle gives four tests that we can give ourselves in order to determine whether or not we have been born again.

1. *The test of obedience.*—"By this we know that we have come to know Him, if we keep His commandments" (2:3). The one who claims to know Christ and yet who walks in willful sin is lying according to 1 John 2:4.

2. *The test of brotherly love.*—"The one who says he is in the light and yet hates his brother is in the darkness until now" (2:9).

3. *The test of confession.*—"Every spirit that confesses that Jesus Christ has come in the flesh is from God; and every spirit that does not confess Jesus is not from God; and this is the spirit of the antichrist, of which you have heard that it is coming, and now it is already in the world" (4:2-3).

4. *The test of the Spirit.*—"By this we know that we abide in Him and He in us, because He has given us of His Spirit" (4:13).

This is John's fourfold method of assuring the hearts of believers. He never mentioned remembering an experience or remembering the words of a prayer. Believers assure their hearts by observing their lives. Their lives produce fruit. Sin does not dominate them. They love the brethren. They believe that Jesus Christ is the eternal Son of God. They have the inward testimony of the Holy Spirit that they are children of God.

Paul also emphasized the testimony of the Holy Spirit. In his detailed analysis of the work of the Holy Spirit in the life of the believer in Romans 8, Paul wrote:

> For all who are being led by the Spirit of God, these are sons of God. For you have not received a spirit of slavery leading to fear again, but you have received a spirit of

adoption as sons by which we cry out, 'Abba! Father!' The Spirit Himself bears witness with our spirit that we are children of God" (Rom. 8:14-16).

This witness is the powerful, internal, and subjective influence of the Holy Spirit that testifies to our sonship in Christ. D. M. Lloyd-Jones, speaking of the testimony of the Holy Spirit, wrote that "the highest form of assurance is the immediate assurance that is given by the Spirit Himself."[9]

Peter used much the same method as John. He encouraged readers to "be all the more diligent to make certain about His calling and choosing you; for as long as you practice these things, you will never stumble" (2 Pet. 1:10). What are "these things" that assure believers of their calling and election? Second Peter 1:5-8 calls upon Christians to have:

• Faith,
• Moral excellence,
• Knowledge,
• Self-control,
• Perseverance,
• Godliness,
• Brotherly kindness,
• and Christian love.

Peter reasoned that these fruits will assure the hearts of believers and make their calling and election sure. In Peter, as in the teaching of Paul and John, there is no mention of remembering an initial experience or remembering the words of a prayer.

MacArthur was right in saying, "Genuine assurance comes from seeing the Holy Spirit's transforming work in one's life, not from clinging to the memory of some experience."[10]

Let us be biblical in handling the important issue of security and assurance. Praying a prayer—even using the right words—does not assure that one is born again. One can mouth the words of a saving confession, "Jesus is Lord," and not truly be saved. As Paul argues in 1 Corinthians 12:3, "No one can say 'Jesus is Lord,' except by the Holy Spirit." The false Christians in Matthew 7:22 called Jesus "Lord," but their lives made it clear that Christ had never really become their Lord and that they had never received His transforming spirit of grace.

To conclude, the biblical way of assuring our hearts is something like the following: I ask myself, "Do I really believe that Jesus Christ died on the cross for my sins? Do I really believe that He was buried and raised the third day, and that He is the exalted Lord of heaven and earth? Do I want Him to be my Lord? Do I see in my life the fruit of the Holy Spirit? Do I long for purity? Do I love the people of God? Does the Holy Spirit bear witness with my spirit? Is there the inward cry, 'Abba! Father!', (the cry of devotion to Father God)? Am I continuing to grow in grace and in the knowledge of Christ?"

This is the biblical way of assuring our hearts. The issue is not whether we have to persevere and do certain works to be saved. The issue is that God is producing fruit in the life of those who are genuinely saved. If that fruit is not present, then any assurance experienced is false assurance. Real assurance is based upon the observation in one's life of the grace of God revealed in the character of the professing believer.

Let us not offer to people a superficial assurance based upon a shallow decision that has not produced a changed life.

1. Walter J. Chantry, *Today's Gospel* (Carlisle, Pa.: The Banner of Truth Trust, 1970), 73.

2. August H. Francke, "If and How One May Be Certain that One Is a Child of God," *Pietists: Selected Writings,* The Classics of Western Spirituality, ed. Peter C. Erb (Ramsey, N.J.: Paulist Press, 1983), 146.

3. Lewis S. Chafer, *Grace* (Wheaton: Van Kampen Press, 1922), 26.

4. Zane C. Hodges, *The Gospel Under Siege* (Dallas: Redención Viva, 1981), 48.

5. Chafer, *Grace,* 66-67.

6. C. H. Spurgeon, *The Metropolitan Tabernacle Pulpit,* vol. XIX (Pasadena, Tex.: Pilgrim Publications, 1971), 43.

7. R. C. Sproul, *Pleasing God* (Wheaton: Tyndale House Publishers, 1988), 22.

8. Ibid.

9. D. Martyn Lloyd-Jones, *The Puritans: Their Origins and Successors* (Carlisle, Pa.: The Banner of Truth Trust, 1987), 187.

10. John F. MacArthur, Jr., *The Gospel According to Jesus* (Grand Rapids: Zondervan Publishing House, 1988), 23.

The Challenge of Christian Growth

Now regeneration is a transaction in which the moral nature is so changed that one can never again rest in a life of sin.

—Walter Thomas Conner[1]

Therefore Christ justifies no one whom he does not at the same time sanctify. These benefits are joined together by an everlasting and indissoluble bond, so that those whom he illumines by his wisdom, he redeems; those whom he redeems, he justifies; those whom he justifies, he sanctifies.

—John Calvin[2]

When Jesus comes again we shall be like him. We shall be perfect, free from sin, and full of love. And our whole Christian life now is a movement towards that goal.

—Stephen H. Travis[3]

8 The Challenge of Christian Growth

Several statements can be made about everyone who has come to Christ for salvation.

1. *All who come to Christ for salvation have repented of sin.* They are committed to Jesus as Lord and Savior. They are willing for Christ to take over their lives.

2. *All who come to Christ for salvation are at first immature.* Ingrained patterns of thinking need to be reprogrammed. Unbiblical convictions must be challenged and changed. Adults have developed habits and perhaps strongholds of sinful behavior that must be broken. Their initial commitment to Christ guarantees that new Christians have the basic spiritual tools to deal with these issues, but there is spiritual conflict ahead, nevertheless.

3. *All who have come to Christ for salvation must grow.* They must change their thought patterns. New Christians must experience continuous spiritual growth in order to change thought patterns and break bad habits.

Is such growth inevitable? Or can Christians remain babies all their lives? Is there some relationship between *regeneration* (the theological term for the new birth) and *sanctification* (the theological term for Christian growth)?

Sanctification

Sanctification has been defined in the past as "the work of God's free grace, whereby we are renewed in the whole man after the image of God, and are enabled more and more to die unto sin, and live unto righteousness."[4] E. Y. Mullins defined sanctification as the "attainment of moral character by the Christian through struggle."[5]

Sanctification is the work of the Holy Spirit in believers to make them more and more like Christ. In regeneration believers receive a new nature by the indwelling Holy Spirit. They are born again to a new relationship with God the Father and quickened through repentance and faith to a desire for godliness and holiness. Sanctification is the Holy Spirit's working out progressively what began in regeneration.

Truths About Sanctification

Several truths about sanctification that need to be remembered are:

1. *Sanctification is not an experience.*—The Holiness movement, the Deeper Life movement, and the Neo-Pentecostal movement have all emphasized some supernatural spurt toward sanctification, or perhaps to complete the process. This has been called the second blessing, the baptism of the Holy Spirit, or other names. The Bible emphasis is not on experiences but on living a certain kind of life. Paul called this fighting a good fight of faith (1 Tim. 6:12). He spoke of working out our salvation with fear and trembling (Phil. 2:12). It may be simpler to have an ecstatic experience that eradicates our flesh, but that is not the biblical way. As Martyn Lloyd-Jones wrote, "Holiness is not something to be received in a meeting; it is a life to be lived and to be lived in detail."[6]

Many victims of faulty evangelism are attracted to the second-blessing approach. This seems to be the opinion of Robert L. Hamblin and William H. Stevens:

Eternity magazine reported results of the "Here's Life America" campaign of Campus Crusade. In six metropolitan areas where the survey was conducted, the 178 participating churches reported 26,535 gospel presentations and 4,106 decisions for Christ, of which 525 joined follow-up Bible studies and 125 became church members. That is, 3 percent of the "converts" joined churches. Many, perhaps most, converts become inactive; those who continue are forced to deal with calls to discipleship that depend on their own efforts and strength. Some come to seek a sort of "second blessing" in which they realize that they have accepted Christ as Savior but never as Lord.[7]

Are some who claim a remarkable second experience of grace really meeting the Lord for the first time? They were not evangelized properly and made a shallow commitment to Christ without ever accepting Him as Lord. They experienced no victory in their Christian walk. They were inactive or shallow church members until their "second blessing," which may have been, in fact, their conversion.

2. *Sanctification is an uneven process.*—The Holy Spirit must break habits and patterns of the old life. This happens only gradually. Drinking, smoking, or fornication may be conquered immediately, but the whole pattern of self-centered and sinful behavior dies hard.

Perhaps the most accurate picture of the Christian life ever written was John Bunyan's *Pilgrim's Progress*. Christian walks through the Valley of Humiliation and is wounded by the fiery darts of Apollyon. He passes through Vanity Fair. Giant Despair almost imprisons him in Doubting-Castle. Despite all this, two truths stand out about Christian: (1) he is a pilgrim on a journey, never arriving until he reaches the Celestial City; (2) he is always progressing, never standing still, ever on the way.

3. *Backsliding and failure are possible.*—This is not the ideal. We should never teach new Christians that they may expect to fail the Lord miserably. We must also be honest and admit that some in Scripture "made shipwreck of the faith." Samson was a believer who sinned greatly. Paul informed young Timothy that Demas had forsaken him, "having loved this present world" (2 Tim. 4:10).

Great moral failure is not the only way we backslide, however. Most Christians from time to time feel that they are spiritually stale. Honesty forces most of us to admit now and then that we are making little progress in the Christian life. We feel like the Greek tragic hero named Sisyphus. He was required by the gods to push a boulder to the top of a steep hill only to have the boulder roll back down. Again and again Sisyphus pushed the boulder to the top, only to repeat the cycle. The sincere saint of God may feel like Sisyphus, but in actuality the Holy Spirit is helping the Christian grow, despite our occasional failure and backsliding.

4. *Sinless perfection is not a possibility in this life.*—Christians are freed from the dominion of sin but not from the possibility of committing sins. Why does the New Testament repeatedly admonish us to flee from sin? Because sin is a possibility.

John Wesley taught that Christians can reach a "relative perfection"; he believed the children of God can be perfected in love so that every act is motivated by love for Christ. Charles Finney taught the doctrine of "entire sanctification" by which he meant that "it was the privilege of Christians to live without known sin."[8] It seems, however, that the closer we get to Christ, the greater the moral distance seems between Him and us.

Calvin was right when he wrote that "in the saints, until they are divested of mortal bodies, there is always sin; for in their flesh there resides that depravity of inordinate desiring which contends against righteousness."[9] Luther taught that the believer is both righteous and a sinner at the same time (*simul iustus et peccator*). Believers have a fallen human nature until death. They are righteous before God because of God's act of justification, yet they still carry within them the vestige of fallen humanity, and they struggle with sin throughout life.

5. *Sanctification is inevitable but not automatic.*—This is a paradox. Sanctification is inevitable in that Christians progress in holiness as long as they live. There is no such thing as a Christian who doesn't grow. Just as bearing fruit is the evidence of life, so growth in Christlikeness is the evidence of regeneration.

The inevitability of sanctification is the result of the relationship between regeneration, justification, and sanctification. There is no such thing as justification without sanctification.

Southern Baptist theologian W. T. Conner faulted those who separate the ideas of justification, regeneration, and sanctification by making justification a mere forensic term:

The preaching of such a forensic doctrine—sometimes in popular and one-sided forms—has led to a superficial spiritual life. It has led people to feel that salvation was a transaction in which they might be delivered from the penalty of sin—be declared just—whether they were ever made righteous or not.[10]

Conner taught that justification and sanctification are not to be separated as if God may do one and not the other.

The Reformers, likewise, argued that justification implied sanctification. Luther wrote against the antinomians, who taught that sanctification is not the necessary consequence of justification.[11] Some modern dispensationalists have done virtually the same thing by separating Christ as Savior from Christ as Lord. Calvin clearly taught that justification and sanctification cannot be divided:

> Therefore Christ justifies no one whom he does not at the same time sanctify. These benefits are joined together by an everlasting and indissoluble bond, so that those whom he illumines by his wisdom, he redeems; those whom he redeems, he justifies; those whom he justifies, he sanctifies. . . . Do you wish, then, to attain righteousness in Christ? You must first possess Christ; but you cannot possess him without being made partaker in his sanctification, because he cannot be divided into pieces (1 Cor. 1:13).[12]

Sanctification is inevitable because, like conversion, it is the work of God. This is Paul's argument in 1 Corinthians 1:30: "By His doing you are in Christ Jesus, who became to us wisdom from God, and righteousness and sanctification, and redemption."

From start to finish salvation (including regeneration, justification, sanctification, and glorification) is the act of God. That is why Spurgeon could say, "The faith by which we are justified is the faith which produces holiness, and no man is justified by faith which does not also sanctify him, and deliver him from the love of sin."[13]

A straightforward reading of Romans 1-8 is sufficient to reach the conclusion that justification cannot be experienced without sanctification. By faith, Paul teaches, we lay hold of the righteousness of Christ and are justified (Rom. 5:1). Despite the difficulties ahead, believers will persevere in faith and hope because the Holy Spirit fills their hearts with the knowledge of God's love for them (v. 5). The Holy Spirit also gives them a new mind-set, freeing them to please the Lord (8:4-8). Paul never taught that *some* who are justified may also be sanctified. He taught that *all* who are justified are also sanctified by the Holy Spirit: "If anyone does not have the Spirit of Christ, he does not belong" to Christ (v. 9). In other words, justification implies sanctification.

The Bible is equally clear that sanctification requires the cooperation of the Christian. This is the other side of our paradox: sanctification is not automatic. God has determined to fashion us into the likeness of Jesus Christ (Rom. 8:29). Scripture does not teach us to be passive or quietist. We must act.

A few representative Scriptures include the following:

> For this is the will of God, your sanctification; that is, that you abstain from sexual immorality . . . . For God has not called us for the purpose of impurity, but in sanctification . . .

> Now may the God of peace Himself sanctify you entirely; and may your spirit and soul and body be preserved complete, without blame at the coming of our Lord Jesus Christ (1 Thess. 4:3, 7; 5:23).

> Just as He chose us in Him before the foundation of the world, that we should be holy and blameless before Him . . . For by grace you have been saved through faith; and that not of yourselves, it is the gift of God; not as a result of works, that no one should boast. For we are His workmanship, created in Christ Jesus for good works, which God prepared beforehand, that we should walk in them" (Eph. 1:4; 2:8-10).

> But like the Holy One who called you, be holy yourselves
> also in all your behavior; because it is written, "You shall
> be holy, for I am holy" (1 Pet. 1:15-16).

> Therefore, having these promises, beloved, let us
> cleanse ourselves from all defilement of flesh and spirit,
> perfecting holiness in the fear of God (2 Cor. 7:1).

It is obvious from these Scriptures that the Christian has a part in his or her own sanctification. As J. I. Packer has written, "Holiness is both God's gift and his command."[14] This involves a paradox or a seeming antinomy. If sanctification is the work of the Holy Spirit in us, then why should we be concerned about it? The Puritan John Owen noted that the Scriptures which teach we are partakers of the divine nature (2 Pet. 1:4) also teach that we must be diligent to add to our faith the qualities of moral excellence, knowledge, self-control, perseverance, godliness, brotherly kindness, and love (2 Pet. 1:5-7). Owen said that carnal reason may not be able to discern the "consistency between *God's effectual grace* and our *diligent obedience*," but both are true.[15]

As a result, Christians must struggle with temptation. They must mortify their old nature and fight the good fight of faith. They must use the "means of grace," especially Bible reading, worship attendance, and prayer. Even so, any real progress in Christlikeness is the work of the Holy Spirit in us. We are being sanctified because of our union with Christ by His Spirit.

Sanctification is inevitable because the God who saves us will not give up on us. Sanctification is not automatic because we must cooperate with the Holy Spirit in this process. Our failure to maintain the tension between these two apparent contradictory statements has severely weakened the church's walk and witness.

1. Walter T. Conner, *The Gospel of Redemption* (Nashville: Broadman Press, 1973), 188.

2. John Calvin, *Institutes of the Christian Religion,* 3.16.1.

3. Stephen H. Travis, *I Believe in the Second Coming of Jesus* (Grand Rapids: Wm B. Eerdmans Publishing Co., 1982), 215.

4. *Westminster Shorter Catechism,* Question 35.

5. Edgar Y. Mullins, *The Christian Religion in Its Doctrinal Expression* (Valley Forge: The Judson Press, 1964), 420.

6. D. Martyn Lloyd-Jones, *Studies in the Sermon on the Mount,* Two volumes in one (Grand Rapids: Wm. B. Eerdmans Publishing Co., 1971), 289, vol. 1.

7. Robert L. Hamblin and William H. Stephens, *The Doctrine of Lordship* (Nashville: Convention Press, 1990), 69.

8. *The Autobiography of Charles G. Finney,* ed. Helen Wessel (Minneapolis: Bethany House Publishers, 1977), 186.

9. Calvin, *Insitutes of the Christian Religion,* 3.3.10.

10. Conner, *The Gospel of Redemption,* 177.

11. See "Sanctification," in *New Dictionary of Theology* (n.p., n.d.), 615.

12. Calvin, *Institutes of the Christian Religion,* 3.16.1.

13. C. H. Spurgeon, *The Metropolitan Tabernacle Pulpit,* vol. XVII (Pasadena, Tex.: Pilgrim Publications, 1971), 99-100.

14. J. I. Packer, *Keep in Step with the Spirit* (Old Tappan: Fleming H. Revell Co., 1984), 96.

15. John Owen, *The Holy Spirit* (Grand Rapids: Sovereign Grace Publishers, 1971), 394.

Church Discipline

People are attracted to churches where real discipline exists. But the real irony is that we have assumed that growing church membership means that the ranks of the Christian army are growing whereas the number of combat troops is in fact shrinking. Churches have become hospitals where sin-sick souls are given aspirin and entertainment to distract them from the diseases of their souls. God forgive us, we are more concerned with numbers than with holiness.

—John White and Ken Blue[1]

The Church ought to know, however, that this absence of any kind of Church discipline inevitably gives the impression that to belong or not to belong to the Church comes to the same thing in the end, and makes no difference in practical life.

—Emil Brunner[2]

Quite frankly, I can think of few more powerful proofs that Christianity is the champion of purity than the compassionate efforts of one family member helping another brother or sister get out of the ditch.

—Charles R. Swindoll[3]

9 Church Discipline

The doctrine of easy believism is a serious threat to the health and vitality of the church. Since it calls for no commitment, it may fill the church with the unrepentant and the unregenerate. As a result, God's true saints will be discouraged by the corruption of the church's membership. The church will be a poor witness to the world of God's transforming grace. Therefore, it is important to call churches back, not only to doctrinal soundness but also to discipline.

The Reformers recovered both the doctrine of salvation and the doctrine of the church as a disciplined community. Calvin wrote:

> Discipline is like a bridle to restrain and tame those who rage against the doctrine of Christ; or like a spur to arouse those of little inclination; and also sometimes like a father's rod to chastise mildly and with the gentleness of Christ's Spirit those who have more seriously lapsed.[4]

The great Reformed confessions, such as the Augsburg, the first Scots, the Belgic, the Heidelberg, and the Westminster, all taught that discipline is essential to the well-being of the church. Some Reformers, like Bucer, believed that discipline was one of the *notae* or marks by which the church is recognized as the church.[5]

Baptists have likewise emphasized the church as a disciplined community of faith. The London Confession of 1644 (Articles 42 and 43) and the Second London Confession of 1677 (Articles 26, 27, and 30) prescribe either formal excommunication or withholding of the Lord's Supper as means of disciplining errant members.[6]

The article by Floyd Patterson on "Discipline" in the *Encyclopedia of Southern Baptists* states:

> The books of discipline, which once were in wide use among Baptists in America, ordinarily have opening chapters on church doctrine, church officers, conditions of reception into membership, and the duties of members. These are followed by chapters on how to deal directly with members who, after right instruction and credible profession, have fallen into sin. These measures are "commonly called Church-Censures, which differ in their nature according to the Nature and Degree of Offence."[7]

Southern Baptist theologian John Newport has written that discipline is one of the three marks of a true church.

> The church is not a chance collection of people, but a community of believers called and united together by the grace of God—a covenant people. Christian believers, therefore, accept responsibility for each other and agree to exercise such discipline as is necessary to remain faithful to God's covenant (1 Cor. 5:1-5). The church takes seriously the Bible's instructions to warn, rebuke, exhort, encourage, and build one another up in love.[8]

Newport has accurately captured the spirit of early Baptists who considered the church a holy society of individuals who came together in covenant and submitted their individual lives to the discipline of the body. This note has been missing in the teaching of Baptist churches for many years. Stephen M. Haines studied Southern Baptist church discipline between 1880-1939 and concluded that three factors contributed to its decline: abuses in the past, the twentieth-century spirit of individualism and optimism, and the incorporation of methods and values of the business world by the church.[9]

Even so, church discipline has never been a popular subject. A seventeenth-century Reformed pastor, Richard Baxter, lamented:

Nowhere can almost a faithful minister set up the unques-
tionable discipline of Christ, or put back the most scandal-
ous impenitent sinners from the communion of the Church
and participation of the sacraments, but the most of the
people rail at them and revile them; as if these ignorant
careless souls were wiser than their teachers, or than God
Himself."[10]

In his book *The Official Rule Book for the New Church Game*,
Baptist pastor Ken Hemphill offers three reasons why churches
today have neglected the issue of discipline.
First, we do not place a sufficiently high premium on our
church fellowship. Second, we do not fully appreciate the
tragic results of our personal sins on the corporate life of
the church. Third, we are not willing to pay the high cost
of personal involvement.[11]

Hemphill believes that an undisciplined church will not attract
the world to Christ because it will not manifest Christ's saving
power.
Darrell Robinson has used the analogy of the human body to
explain church discipline: "For a person to have a healthy body,
discipline is necessary. Even so, for a local church to be a
healthy body of Christ, discipline is essential."[12]

Church Discipline in the New Testament

Robinson believed that the biblical materials on discipline can
be divided into three categories:
1. *Formative discipline.*
Basing his view on texts such as Hebrews 10:23-25 and Colos-
sians 3:16, Robinson noted that formative discipline includes the
"normal attention" that should be given to members, especially
encouragement of their spiritual growth.
2. *Restorative discipline.*
Robinson based his second category in Scriptures like 2 Thessalonians 3:14-15, Galatians 6:1-2, Matthew 5:23-24 and 18:15.
When believers become negligent in attendance or active in sin-

ful behavior, they are vulnerable to being overcome by their sinfulness. It is necessary, therefore, that the church take immediate action to ensure that the disease does not spread throughout these Christian's lives and throughout the church.

Churches are in trouble, Robinson believed, when they neglect clear texts such as Galatians 6:1-2.

What is often done when a member becomes spiritually diseased and backslides? Nothing! He is often ignored, hoping that the problem or the person goes away. Sometimes he is attacked and condemned. He is down and kicked while he is down. Thus, he becomes more defeated.[13]

Robinson emphasized that restorative discipline is redemptive and compassionate in its design.

3. *Amputative discipline.*
This is Darrel Robinson's term for what is normally called "excommunication." He cited five biblical grounds for amputation:
- Immorality (1 Corinthians 5:4-5)
- Heresy (Titus 3:10)
- False professions (1 John 2:19-20)
- Rebellion against church authority (Matthew 18:17)
- Hypocrisy (Acts 5).[14]

Benefits of Church Discipline

The reasons for practicing discipline are obvious.

To protect the church.—Each church needs to protect itself from the corrupting influences of sin, heresy, and schism. In 1 Corinthians 5:6-7, Paul argued that sin in the fellowship is like leaven in a lump of dough: it spreads until the whole lump is affected by the leaven. He admonished the church to "clean out the old leaven" (in this case, immorality) so that the church can worship the Lord in "sincerity and truth" (vv. 7-8). Paul did not argue for censuring a church member because he disliked the person but because he valued the glory of Christ and the good of the entire congregation more than the temporal happiness of an individual member.

On this point, Ken Hemphill has written:
Sin compromises fellowship, it destroys *koinnia,* and thus,

in the long run, it affects our ministry. Therefore, to appreciate the value of church discipline we must treasure church fellowship. We must value our fellowship so highly that when it is interrupted or lost, we persistently seek its restoration.[15]

To strengthen the church's influence.—We must not underestimate the deleterious effects of sin on the church's ability to influence its community for Christ. In his book *Why Conservative Churches Are Growing*, Dean N. Kelley said that discipline or "strictness" is a characteristic of nearly all significant and society-transforming religious movements. He wrote, "*A group with evidence of social strength will proportionately show traits of strictness; a group with traits of leniency will proportionately show evidences of social weakness rather than strength.*"[16]

To help the offender.—Church discipline needs to be seen as an act of love, not of malice or of anger. Love does not allow a church member to sin with impunity, becoming hardened and insensitive to the love of Christ and the fellowship of believers. Loving and restorative discipline is costly and sometimes painful. It requires personal involvement. Even so, loving discipline is essential for the good of the church and the good of the individual church member. When an errant member is not disciplined, he or she may become puffed up and resentful of the church and will become "like a spoiled child who does not receive guidance or discipline from his parents."[17]

The Process of Disciplining

The steps involved in disciplining an unfaithful church member involved in immorality, heresy, or schism are the following:

1. *Rebuke by one Christian.*—The church member who knows of a fallen brother or sister should first go to that sinning saint and lovingly rebuke him or her in Christ's name (Gal. 6:1; Matt. 18:15). Hopefully, the matter will end there, and the sinning saint will be reclaimed through repentance.

2. *Rebuke by two or three Christians.*—If this does not work, however, the second step is for the concerned member to take

one or two others to see the erring member (Matt. 18:16). This will indicate the gravity of the situation. The hope still is that the brother or sister will become repentant, will forsake sin, and be restored to full fellowship of the church.

3. *Consideration by the church.*—If the second step fails, the third step then is to take the matter to the church (Matt. 18:17). The church member has indicated an obstinate and unrepentant heart. In this case, the issue needs to be taken to the church for serious prayer and intercession.

At this point, Paul's injunctions in 1 Corinthians 5:11 and 1 Thessalonians 3:14-15 become operative. Members are to withhold Christian fellowship from those who call themselves Christians but who are living in sin. They are not to associate with them or even to eat with them. Historically, Baptists have interpreted this to include suspension from the Lord's Table and the privilege of voting.[18]

4. *Excommunication.*—The final step is the one that the others were designed to make unnecessary. It is the step of excommunication, or what Ken Hemphill called "quarantine"[19] (1 Cor. 4:5; Matt. 18:17). Even this radical step of excommunication has a redemptive purpose! It is to bring a sinning saint to his or her senses and to lead the person to repentance.

On the other hand, it is possible that the church member is unsaved. This drastic action of the church may serve to awaken the person to his or her need for Christ, once the person is put outside the fellowship of the believing community.

One of my New Testament professors at New Orleans Seminary shared an experience from his own ministry that illustrates this point. In one congregation where the professor had served as pastor, there was a man who prided himself on being a church leader. Even so, this man was grossly sinful and continued unrepentant for long while. Some leaders of the church urged him to change his life-style, but he refused. Finally the matter came before the congregation, and the man was excommunicated.

Months later the excluded church member came to church and made a profession of faith. He told the church something to this effect:

> While I was a member of the church I knew that my life-style was not as it should be. I often felt convicted that I was wrong, and sometimes I even questioned whether I was saved. Then I would say, "Of course, I'm saved. I'm a member of the such-and-such Baptist church and an officer in that church. I must be saved." Then when the church took the drastic action that it did and excommunicated me, I continued in my sin. One day I began to feel guilty for what I was doing. I began to question whether I was saved. Then I went back to my old argument: "Certainly I must be saved. I'm a member of the such-and-such Baptist Church." That's when I remembered that I was no longer a member of the church. That loving church had disfellow-shipped me, and I could no longer claim membership. The Holy Spirit spoke to my heart and told me that I was not a child of God. I had never been born again. That's when I repented and gave my heart to Christ.

Of course, not all excommunications have such beautiful results, but that is their intention.

The Undisciplined Church

An undisciplined church will not only become impure, but it will become a discouraged church. The true saints will lose heart when they see the low level of spirituality resulting from lost church members and undisciplined saints. A disciplined and loving congregation radiates the personality of Christ and attracts a lost world.

R. C. Sproul has an important word for churches that take seriously their responsibility to discipline:

> The discipline of the church is part of her priestly duty and must be carried out in a priestly manner if people are to be highly valued. God Himself, like the prodigal's father, lets people depart from Him when they are determined to go, but He lets them go with tears.[20]

Churches that decide to return to the biblical pattern of disciplined church life need to be aware that recently a number of lawsuits have been brought against churches that have disciplined their members. A number of books and articles give churches legal advice on how to stay out of court, or if sued, how to handle the situation.[21]

Some pastors and churches may be reluctant to follow the biblical pattern of church discipline because they fear it will hurt numberical growth. Two things need to be said about this:

• We need to repent of our attitude that a big church is more important than a holy church.

• There is growing evidence that a truly disciplined church will be a growing church.

Church growth specialist Peter Wagner has concluded that, in both the East and West, in Third World countries, and highly industrialized nations, "there is a positive correlation between corrective church discipline and church growth."[22] The ultimate concern, however, should be our obedience to Scripture.

In his book *Beyond Forgiveness: The Healing Touch of Church Discipline*, Pastor Don Baker told a touching real-life drama of redemptive discipline in a local church.[23] Anyone who doubts that the dual concerns for a holy church and a loving church can be balanced should read this story of loving confrontation, accountability, and restoration.

1. John White and Ken Blue, *Healing the Wounded: The Costly Love of Church Discipline* (Downers Grove, Ill.: Inter-Varsity Press, 1985), 34.

2. Emil Brunner, *The Divine Imperative* (Philadelphia: Westminster Press, 1937), 558-59.

3. Charles R. Swindoll, *Strengthening Your Grip* (Waco, Tex.: Word Books, 1982), 67.

4. John Calvin, *Institutes of the Christian Religion*, 4.12.1.

5. John T. McNeill, *The History and Character of Calvinism* (London: Oxford University Press, 1954), 80-81.

6. See William Lumpkin, *Baptist Confessions of Faith* (Valley Forge: The Judson Press, 1969), 168, 286-87, 293.

7. Floyd Patterson, "Discipline," *Encyclopedia of Southern Baptists,* vol. 1 (Nashville: Broadman Press, 1958), 365.

8. John P. Newport, *What Is Christian Doctrine?* (Nashville: Broadman Press, 1984), 134.

9. Stephen M. Haines, "Southern Baptist Church Discipline, 1880-1939," *Baptist*

History and Heritage 20 (April 1985, no. 2): 14-27.

10. Richard Baxter, *Call to the Unconverted* (Grand Rapids: Sovereign Grace Publishers, 1971), 5-6.

11. Ken Hemphill, *The Official Rule Book for the New Church Game* (Nashville: Broadman Press, 1990, 139.

12. Darrell W. Robinson, *Total Church Life* (Nashville: Broadman Press, 1985), 59.

13. Ibid., 60.

14. Ibid., 63-64.

15. Hemphill, *New Church Game,* 140.

16. Dean N. Kelley, *Why Conservative Churches Are Growing* (New York: Harper and Row Publishers, Inc., 1972), 86.

17. Robinson, *Total Church Life,* 65.

18. *Encyclopedia of Southern Baptists,* 365, vol. 1.

19. Hemphill, *New Church Game,* 144.

20. R. C. Sproul, *In Search of Dignity* (Ventura: Regal Books, 1983), 183.

21. See Lynn R. Buzzard and Thomas Brandon, *Church Discipline in the Courts* (Tyndale House Publishers, 1987); J. Carl Laney, "Church Discipline Without a Lawsuit," *Christianity Today,* November 9, 1984, 76; and Leslie B. Flynn, *When the Saints Come Storming In* (Wheaton: Victor Books, 1988), 115-17.

22. Cited by White and Blue in *Healing the Wounded,* 72.

23. Don Baker, *Beyond Forgiveness: The Healing Touch of Church Discipline* (Portland: Multnomah Press, 1984, n.p.)

New Testament Evangelism

We don't have to call in TV celebrities and athletic personalities to put the gospel over. We're trying to fix up something that doesn't need fixing up. We're trying to gild the lily and paint the sunset, hobnob with Sodom, and get chummy with Gomorrah. You don't have to go to the love-ins to find out what the hippies are thinking, or drink gingerale at the country clubs to find out what that crowd's thinking.

—Vance Havner[1]

God packed into the personality of Jesus Christ all the charms of deity and humanity and made Him the chief among ten thousand—the one altogether lovely, the Rose of Sharon. He tops all winners in time and eternity. He is distinctly the world's chiefest soul-winner and evangelist. He "came to seek and save that which was lost" (Luke 19:10). He is the model for all winners. His example in method, spirit, message, doctrine, for all time will be the standard for all who seek to bring men to God—"Follow me and I will make you fishers of men" (Matt. 4:19). Our guarantee of success is found in our approximation to His method. To all evangelists He sounds out "Folow me."

—L. R. Scarborough[2]

10 New Testament Evangelism

The primary task of the church is to reach the lost for Christ. The Son of God took flesh in the person of Jesus Christ and died on the cross to save lost souls from hell. The church may do many other important things, but her primary task is *evangelism*.

Evangelism, furthermore, is every Christian's duty. L. R. Scarborough wrote:

This divine obligation rests without exception upon the heart and conscience of every Spirit-born child of God. The Christian receives the essence of this obligation and call in the same bundle with his salvation. Regeneration demands reproduction in kind."[3]

Jesus said, "Follow Me, and I will make you become fishers of men" (Mark 1:17). Wayne Dehoney is reported to have said, "Jesus calls us to be fishers of men, but we have become keepers of the aquarium." Too often we have substituted church work for the work of the church, which is evangelism. Good church work is sometimes the enemy of the best. It is good to go to many Bible studies and participate in the corporate life of the church, but we disobey Christ if, in doing these things, we do not follow our Lord's command to reach others for Him. It is crucial that we motivate and equip believers to evangelize.

A shallow gospel produces shallow Christians at best, lost church members at worst. Our church rolls have the names of thousands who never attend services or serve the Lord in any way. For kingdom purposes they are nonexistent. Many, if not most of them, are lost. It is important that pastors, evangelists, and churches examine not only the content of the gospel they are preaching but also the methods they are using. Possibly the high attrition rate of professed Christians results from contemporary styles of evangelism.

Hollywood Evangelism

In our legitimate concern to reach people, we have often resorted to show-business techniques. We call on movie stars, athletes, and other public personalities to tell how Jesus made them rich, famous, or successful. Many people may be more attracted to the glitter of success than to the Lord Jesus Christ. Shockingly, many celebrities used in evangelistic campaigns have never separated themselves from worldly and sinful practices. Vance Havner once wrote:

> Television actors appear in evangelistic meetings one week and filthy shows the next. Dance programs feature hymns. Gospel rock and Christian combos and hippie evangelists abound. Jazz bands play in staid old sanctuaries, and the church that used to go to the jungle is now seeing the jungle brought into the church. . . . There's a delusion going around today, even in evangelical and fundamental circles sometimes, that we must be entertained at church. Christianity has come all the way from an experience to a performance."[4]

It is certainly not wrong to use the testimony of a successful person, but we must be sure that the person's private life is consistent with the New Testament. When we promote someone in this way we are recommending that person's life-style. We are holding up the person as a model of Christian virtue and character. Before presenting someone to the public, we pastors need to ask ourselves, Is this the kind of Christian that I want my people to be?

We too quickly promote well-known personalities who have made professions of faith. We are so hungry to use their notoriety for the cause of Christ that we promote them before they are tested. For instance, Larry Flynt, publisher of *Hustler* magazine, professed faith a few years ago and was immediately brought into the evangelical spotlight. He did not break with *Hustler*, however. We need to heed the admonition of Paul to young Timothy: "Do not lay hands upon anyone too hastily and thus share responsibility for the sins of others" (1 Tim. 5:22).

Hollywood evangelism also transforms preachers into celebrities. James A. Stewart observed over thirty years ago, "Gospel preachers who used to be merely humble servants of God, exalting a great and mighty Lord Jesus, are *now glamourized into celebrities*. They are advertised as 'colossal,' and 'famous,' and 'terrific,' and 'charming,' and even as 'Gospel artists.'"[5]

Television and the media have created an appetite in America for celebrities, and many churches have obliged them by calling pastors who are more skilled in public relations than in preaching the gospel, pastors who are prettier than they are holy, pastors who are better mixers and hail-fellows-well-met than men of prayer.

As a pastor I always want to draw crowds and build my church. Yet this desire for growth itself can be idolatrous. We dare not sacrifice principle, even for numbers. It took months before the Jerusalem church accepted Paul after his conversion. Today we would have immediately set up the gospel tent or rented a stadium and permitted Paul to give his testimony. The church in Jerusalem knew there was too much at stake. Paul had first to be proved. Only after earning his spurs, so to speak, did Paul have the right to stand publicly and declare his confidence in the gospel of Christ.

Americans have often criticized Baptists in South America and other countries who require probationary periods before one accepting candidates for baptism and church membership. Their practices may be more realistic than ours. On the mission field Christian leaders know what we have forgotten: persons can profess faith without leaving their old gods, their old religion, and their old faith. They also know that true followers of Christ will stick it out long enough to be baptized, even if there is a waiting period.

In our country, we spend weeks and months after an evangelistic campaign encouraging those who have made decisions to be baptized. It seems to me that a genuine convert will want to be baptized. (To be sure, some youth and children have to await their parents' consent.) Many resist baptism because their shallow decision was produced by the questionable methods of Hollywood evangelism. Much of Hollywood evangelism is rooted in a holy desire to reach souls for Christ, but much of it also results from our success mentality and our lust for numbers. Pastors judge one another by the numbers that they produce. If a super-star gets the numbers in, if a performer-athlete draws crowds, if Miss America brings in people, then we call on them.

Even evangelists themselves have not escaped this tyranny of numbers. According to Lewis Sperry Chafer:

This unfruitful condition of the church has created a great temptation for the evangelist to be superficial in his aim and undertakings. His reputation, and often his remuneration, are dependent upon apparent results; for many pastors and churches have been trained to a vision of quantity in results rather than to a due regard for quality.[6]

Another driving force behind Hollywood evangelism may be our feelings of insecurity in the face of the many attacks against Christianity. This is Charles Colson's assessment of the situation:

Why can't Christians see that all this hoopla about celebrities merely reveals our own insecurity, as if we must prove that God still works by putting on display the latest convert? The strength of our faith rests not upon the dramatic turnaround of the corrupt politician or depraved pornographer, but upon the truth of God's word."[7]

Consumer Evangelism

Much evangelism in America has bowed before the shrines of success and prosperity. Religion in this country has sanctified the American dream and sacramentalized prosperity. Our slogans are: "The devil's kids shouldn't have all the money," and, "You're a child of the King, so live like one." These slogans sound all too good to a nation with an insatiable lust for the good life. "Gutter-to-grace testimonies have become rags-to-riches testimonials, and fantastic expenditure is poured into showcase projects which are flagships for the showman commanders of the new empires."[8]

What would Jesus say to this generation? Probably the same thing he said to His own generation: "What does it profit a man to gain the whole world, and forfeit his own soul?" (Mark 8:36); or, "It is easier for a camel to go through the eye of a needle than for a rich man to enter the kingdom of heaven" (Matt. 19:24). Paul would likely tell our preachers: "Instruct those who are rich in this present world not to be conceited or to fix their hope on the uncertainty of riches, but on God, who richly supplies us with all things to enjoy" (1 Tim. 6:17); or James would say, "Come now, you rich, weep and howl for your miseries which are coming upon you. Your riches have rotted and your garments have become moth-eaten. Your gold and your silver have rusted; and their rust will be a witness against you and will consume your flesh like fire" (5:1-3).

Consumer evangelism says we can have Jesus and the good life too. No, it says it even more bluntly: the key to the good life is Jesus. What is understood as "the good life"? Not forgiveness of sins, inner peace, and a home in heaven. It means having the goods right now in this life. Like good pragmatists, the only test that most Americans apply to this doctrine is: Does it work? Does it make preachers successful? Does it fill the pews? Does it pay the rent? Yes, but does consumer evangelism make true disciples?

Psychologized Evangelism

Fad chasers that we are, the religious entrepreneurs and kingdom builders have inevitably harnessed the growing quasi-science of psychology. So effective has this approach become that most churchgoers today would consider it heresy to suggest that the concepts of self-love and self-esteem are not biblical. We have bought into the idea that our greatest problem is an inferiority complex or some other psychologized description of the human predicament.

I am not criticizing the study of psychology nor the critically detached use of psychology. I am criticizing the slavish preoccupation with and servitude to psychology and psychiatry. Charles Templeton said it years ago: "Many a minister hardly dares to say anything about human behavior unless he looks for approval to a psychiatrist."[9]

Low View of God

As I see it, there are three salient characteristics of the psychologized gospel. First, there is a low view of God. Older theologies ranked holiness as God's primary and basic attribute. Holiness meant not only His moral purity but His moral and spiritual transcendence, His "wholly otherness," an emphasis that neoorthodoxy rescued from the wreckage of nineteenth-century liberalism.

Recently, there is a growing discontent with this absolute otherness of the divine nature. An emphasis on the transcendence of God has been replaced by an emphasis on His immanence. Accordingly, the primary attribute of God is said to be love, not His holiness. Nineteenth-century liberals were accused of trying to "discover God by saying 'man' in a loud voice." Twentieth-century psychological evangelists tell us that we can discover ourselves by saying "God" in a loud voice.

"When we are adopted as children of God, the core of our life changes from shame—to self-esteem.

And we can pray, "Our Father in heaven, honorable is *our* name."

So, the foundation is laid for us to feel good about ourselves! The stage is set for important divine marching orders![10]

There you have it! The primary purpose to worship God is so that we can feel good about ourselves and recognize that we have an honorable name.

High View of Ourselves

The second characteristic of psychologized evangelism is a *high view of ourselves*. The Scriptures teach that humans are the apex of creation and bear the image of God. The Bible also teaches that we are fallen creatures, sinners by nature and by practice, and that without moral and spiritual regeneration we will remain rebels and egocentric ingrates.

According to the psychologized gospel of the "new reformation," the emphasis in preaching should be the dignity of the person. Transactional Analysis and the slogan "I'm Okay, You're Okay" has invaded the church. The greatest sin for the preacher today is making someone feel guilty. The preacher's task, it is said, is to deal with the neuroses and brokenness of people's lives. No one should be called a sinner.

Recently I was walking through a mall and saw a display of T-shirts for sale. On the back of one T-shirt was a picture of Jesus Christ on the cross with these words: "If I'm okay and you're okay, explain this."

The goal of the psychologized gospel is not to lead men and women to become humble servants of the Most High God. Rather, the psychologized gospel teaches men and women how to love themselves, how to experience the dignity of their own lives, and how to have self-esteem.

As one of the prophets of the movement has written:
What is that basic flaw ? I believe it is the failure to proclaim the gospel in a way that can satisfy every person's deepest need—one's spiritual hunger for glory. Rather than glorify God's highest creation—the human being—Christian liturgies, hymns, prayers, and scriptural interpretations have often insensitively and destructively offended the dignity of the person. The human ego has been labeled as the ultimate sin, when, in fact, it is the mark of the image of God within people."[11]

Weak View of Sin

The third characteristic of the psychologized gospel is a *weak view of sin*. The Reformers denounced sin as rebellion against God. According to the gospel of the new reformation, sin is simply the absence of total trust; original sin means that "we are all born with a negative self-image, an inferiority complex, if you please."[12]

Alongside this psychologized definition of sin is the prevalence of the medical model in describing the human condition. Sin is a *disease*. We now talk about addictions in such a way as almost to exonerate people from responsibility for their behavior. If a famous baseball player is caught sleeping around with a number of women, his excuse is that he is "a sexual addict." Obviously, if sin is an addiction, then we cannot be held responsible for our behavior.

The gospel of self-esteem wants men and women to experience peace without being confronted with the awful reality of Calvary. If the cross means anything, it means that we are guilty sinners who are guilty of deicide. We can never exalt ourselves by dethroning God. We cannot close the gap between a holy God and sinful persons. We only make ourselves contented sinners who still need to be brought into fellowship with a holy God.

Did Jesus follow the advice of the advocates of psychologized evagelism? Someone once said, "They didn't crucify Christ because He said, 'Behold the lilies of the field, how they grow.' They crucified Him because He insisted on saying, 'Behold the thieves in the temple, how they steal.'"

Over a century ago, Spurgeon remarked:

> Nowadays ministers are to be found who are very fine upon "the dignity of human nature." The "lapsed state of man"—that is the phrase—is sometimes alluded to, but the corruption of our nature, and kindred themes are carefully avoided: . . . . To prophesy smooth things, and to extenuate the evil of our lost estate, is not the way to lead men to Jesus.[13]

Need-Centered Evangelism

In the 1940s, Rabbi Joshua Loth Liebman wrote a book entitled *Peace of Mind*. The book was a phenomenal success and the beginning of what has been called the "peace-of-mind literature." Many similar titles followed from other authors and speakers as Roman Catholic Bishop Fulton J. Sheen. A raw nerve had been discovered in the American psyche, and hundreds of titles claiming to teach us how to live in peace and serenity appeared on the scene. Preachers and evangelists have learned that the way to draw a crowd is to address the felt needs of persons. Speak to their loneliness, their confusion, their lack of peace, their neuroses and their guilt; offer them happiness if they will come to Jesus Christ; present the gospel as a kind of spiritual tranquilizer that will instantaneously remove the disastrous effects of a life lived in rebellion against God.

Typical sermons today deal with subjects such as loneliness, stress, and depression. The preacher usually has statistics and data from specialized studies that will help him appear to be an expert. Using illustrations and anecdotes from the literature or from personal experience, the preacher helps the listener identify needs and then presents Christ as the answer.

Of course, this method is not without merit. It appears to me that the happiest people are those who have come to know Jesus Christ. To be sure, those whose sense of guilt is removed can experience a genuine sense of peace. However, the approach is frought with some difficulties. Need-centered evangelism often uses a *shallow analysis of human problems*. People are led to believe that the adulterous husband, the troubled marriage, or some other problem will be taken care of instantaneously if they walk the aisle and make a commitment to Christ. This promises too much. Need-centered evangelism preaches the gospel not primarily as a solution for sinfulness and brokenness but as a way to deal with the *results* of our sinfulness and brokenness—results such as adultery or divorce. Often there is no transition from the hearers' felt needs (stress, depression, anxiety, loneliness, or lack of peace) to the real need (separation from God). If we present the gospel as a tonic for every human ailment, we will attract people for the wrong reasons. They will want Jesus as a panacea for all their problems, not as a Savior from their sins. To be sure, our motives may be good, but we need to make clear that the lost person's real need is forgiveness, that forgiveness requires repentance, and that discipleship is a long, hard life of commitment and sacrifice. Jesus does not promise instant happiness. We will know joy, but the experience of conversion is not necessarily going to put together all the shards of our broken lives immediately.

The Holy Spirit is sovereign in conversion, and many may be saved through need-centered evangelism. I fear that many are making superficial commitments to Christ, expecting Him to take care of the tragic results of their foolish and sinful mistakes while they may not intend to give Him control of their lives. It may even be deceptive to tell person to come to Christ for peace without also explaining that they will face a hard journey. Their marriage may not improve, their children may still be rebels, and they may still be plagued with problems from their past sinful behavior. The most important thing, however, is that they will know Jesus as Savior. He will give them strength to deal with problems and take them to heaven when they die.

Evangelism in the Local Church

The real need of our hour is not seasonal evangelism, which highlights a professional evangelist, nor culturally captive evangelism of the sort we have described above, but *perennial* evangelism. This consistent evangelism takes place when a local church, led by its pastor, commits to the priority of evangelism, subordinating every other church function to the primary mission of reaching people for Christ.

In order to do this, church leaders must work to create what L. R. Scarborough called a "spiritual atmosphere" in the church:

There must be a spiritual, soul-winning atmosphere in a church, in a Sunday school, in a young people's organization, in a woman's organization, in a class of students anywhere, and in our homes, if the best evangelistic results are to be achieved. Cold spiritual atmospheres are death to evangelistic life. . . . As eggs will not hatch in a refrigerator, but only under the warm mother's wing or in a warm incubator, so spiritual life will not germinate or grow in frigid zones. God's leaders in church and Kingdom ought to have this passionate and enthusiastic burning of heart and warmth of soul if they are to see demonstrations of God's saving power."[14]

Local churches have too often given the work of evangelism over to full-time professionals whom they call in to prop up their weak baptism figures. David Watson has spoken to this trend: "The modern pattern of full-time evangelists should perhaps be seen as a necessary second-best due to the failure of the church concerning its continuous and spantaneous evangelistic work."[15]

I believe that Watson has overstated the truth, but he is leaning in the right direction. The biblical pattern of evangelism, as seen in the Book of Acts, is continual, spontaneous, and effective. Evangelism was not the work of the professionals: it was the ministry of every believer. In order for this to happen, churches must develop a passion for souls. Scarborough said:

You ask, what is this passion for souls and how does it manifest itself? It is a heart-longing, both for Christ, his mastership in our lives, his comradeship in our service, and for unsaved men everywhere, that they may be saved from their sins, that they may trained in Christ's service, that they may be organized into God's great conquering army for world-wide redemption."[16]

This may sound old-fashioned. Equipping and motivating God's people to share their faith directly with others may be written off as outmoded or not in good taste, still the gospel is sufficient (Rom. 1:16). It is the wisdom of God (1 Cor. 1:21). The gospel does not need to be propped up by fleshly wisdom, appeals for corroboration from the social sciences, nor authentication from philosophy or psychology.

Hollywood evangelism may draw large crowds; consumer evangelism may make suburban Christians feel better about themselves; psychologized evangelism may help the church to appear relevant; and need-centered evangelism may make the church seem compassionate. In all these approaches, however, the church risks changing the message as well as the method.

What is the real danger? That we consider the simple gospel as inadequate and the crucified Christ as a scandal.

Vance Havner said that the church needs to get out of the novelty business and back into the antique shop.

Spurgeon was once accused of being nothing but an echo of the Puritans. His bold response should encourage us: "I had rather be the echo of truth, than the voice of falsehood."[17]

1. Vance Havner, *Just a Preacher* (Chicago: Moody Press, 1981), 112.

2. H. R. Scarborough, *With Christ After the Lost* (Nashville: The Sunday School Board of the Southern Baptist Convention, 1919), 53.

3. Scarborough, *With Christ After the Lost,* 10.

4. Havner, *Just a Preacher,* 123.

5. James A. Stewart, *Evangelism* (Zachary, La.: Revival Fires Publishers, 1971), 12.

6. Lewis S. Chafer, *True Evangelism* (New York: Gospel Publishing House, 1911), 19-20.

7. Charles W. Colson, *Life Sentence* (Old Tappan, N.J.: Fleming H. Revell Co., 1979), 273.

8. Os Guinness, *The Gravedigger File: Papers on the Subversion of the Modern Church* (Downers Grove: Inter-Varsity Press, 1983), 132.

9. Charles B. Templeton, "Peace of Mind Is Not Enough," *Great Preaching Today,* ed. Alton M. Motter (New York: Harper and Brothers Publishers, 1955), 226.

10. Robert H. Schuller, *Self-Esteem: the New Reformation* (Waco: Word Books, 1982), 69.

11. Schuller, *Self-Esteem,* 31.

12. Ibid., 65.

13. C. H. Spurgeon, *Lectures to My Students* (Grand Rapids: Zondervan Publishing House, 1954, 338.

14. L. R. Scarborough, *A Search for Souls* (Nashville: The Sunday School Board of the Southern Baptist Convention, 1925), 21-22.

15. David Watson, *I Believe in the Church* (London: Hodder and Stoughton, 1978), 259.

16. Scarborough, *A Search for Souls,* 54.

17. C. H. Spurgeon, *An All-Round Ministry: Addresses to Ministers and Students* (London: The Banner of Truth Trust, 1960), 10.

Conclusion

There are important practical implications of our view that though sinlessness is not experienced in this life, it must be our aim. On the one hand, this position means that there need not be great feelings of discouragement, defeat, even despair and guilt when we do sin. But on the other hand, it also means that we will not be overly pleased with ourselves nor indifferent to the presence of sin. For we will faithfully and diligently ask God to overcome completely the tendency toward evil which, like Paul, we find so prevalent within us.

—Millard J. Erickson[1]

Where sin hath the rule, there the Holy Ghost will never dwell. He enters into no soul as his habitation, but at the same instant he dethrones sin, spoils it of its dominion, and takes the rule of the soul into the hand of his own grace. Where he hath effected this work, and brought his adversary into subjection, there he will dwell, though sometimes his habitation be troubled by his subdued enemy.

—John Owen[2]

Conclusion

Over a decade ago I expressed a concern over the issues in this book to a theologian who had written extensively on the church and the Christian life. He told me that, in his view, it would be difficult for a pastor to lead a church to experience the explosive growth of some of the "super churches" if he preached the message of what has been called "lordship salvation." He believed, after observing the fast-growing congregations, that a pastor would have to be more lenient about discipleship and commitment to draw large crowds.

I believe he is only partly correct. Some churches that have grown rapidly by offering the gospel on "bargain-basement" terms. Some preach positive thinking, self-love, and human potential disguised as the gospel.

Yet I believe that my own denomination is seeing the beginning of a new emphasis on holiness, moral purity, and the ministry of the living Christ by His Spirit in the life of believers. Some churches that preach the lordship of Christ are experiencing rapid growth. Within these congregations one experiences a wonderful sense of God's gracious, awesome, and wonderful presence.

This call for preaching Christ's lordship does not come from one who believes smaller is better. In fact, I am pastoring a fast-growing congregation. I want numerical growth. I want to see every person in my town come to know Christ as Lord and Savior.

I do not believe we have to preach a watered-down gospel in order to attract the masses. The Holy Spirit is the supernatural magnet who draws men and women to the Savior. Our job is to preach Christ in all His fullness. We are to articulate all of His commands; we can leave the results to Him.

The real issue is *truth*. I have tried to be true to Scripture, our ultimate authority. I offer this brief book in humility and with the prayer that it will stimulate us to love and good works (Heb. 10:24).

1. Millard J. Erickson, *Christian Theology,* Vol. 3 (Grand Rapids: Baker Book House, 1983), 974.

2. John Owen, *The Holy Spirit* (Grand Rapids: Sovereign Grace Publishers, 1971), 551.